# COUNTING STARS
## *in an*
# EMPTY SKY

## TRUSTING GOD'S PROMISES FOR YOUR IMPOSSIBILITIES

# MICHAEL YOUSSEF

**BakerBooks**

*a division of Baker Publishing Group*
Grand Rapids, Michigan

© 2019 by Leacheal, Inc.

Published by Baker Books
a division of Baker Publishing Group
PO Box 6287, Grand Rapids, MI 49516-6287
www.bakerbooks.com

Printed in the United States of America

Library of Congress Cataloging-in-Publication Data
Names: Youssef, Michael, author.
Title: Counting stars in an empty sky : trusting God's promises for your
    impossibilities / Michael Youssef.
Description: Grand Rapids : Baker Books, a division of Baker Publishing Group,
    2019. | Includes bibliographical references.
Identifiers: LCCN 2018055814 | ISBN 9780801077876 (pbk.)
Subjects: LCSH: Abraham (Biblical patriarch) | God—Faithfulness. | Trust in God. |
    God—Promises.
Classification: LCC BS580.A3 Y68 2019 | DDC 222/.11092—dc23
LC record available at https://lccn.loc.gov/2018055814

19  20  21  22  23  24  25      7  6  5  4  3  2  1

## Counting Stars in an Empty Sky

"In *Counting Starts in an Empty Sky*, Dr. Michael Youssef gives us the strength to believe in God's promises regardless of our circumstances. He encourages us to keep fighting and to keep believing. If you need to find your faith in one of life's challenging seasons, this book is for you."

**Mark Batterson,** *New York Times* bestselling author
of *The Circle Maker* and lead pastor of National
Community Church

## Praise for *Life-Changing Prayers*

"Most of us are ordinary, yet God can use us in extraordinary ways. Michael Youssef reminds us of this lesson through the stories of seven biblical figures whose lives were changed by one important action—prayer. *Life-Changing Prayers* will make you rethink how and why you pray and bring you closer to God in the process."

**Mark Batterson,** *New York Times* bestselling author
of *The Circle Maker* and lead pastor of National
Community Church

"What liberating truth is found within the covers of this new book by Michael Youssef. God uses ordinary people to call down extraordinary results from God through the dynamic medium of prayer. That means He can actually use me . . . and you! Read it, and you will agree with me that this is no ordinary book. It is passionate and penetrating, insightful and inspiring. Read it . . . and reap!"

**Dr. O. S. Hawkins,** president and CEO of Guidestone
Financial Resources and author of the bestselling
*Joshua Code* and the entire Code series

"This book is addressed to ordinary people, challenging them to pray 'life-changing' prayers. Because I consider myself ordinary, I like this book. It is written for me. This book challenges a need in my heart to pray. If you consider yourself an ordinary Christian, Michael Youssef can lift your intercession to a higher level of effectiveness."

Elmer L. Towns, cofounder and vice president
of Liberty University

"Dr. Youssef's latest book is a most practical and encouraging book on prayer. I kept thinking of William Cowper's words as I read it: 'Satan trembles when he sees the weakest saint upon his knees.' After you read Michael's book, you will want to buy copies to give to every young Christian you know. And yet it will equally encourage every mature Christian as well, because we all have much to learn about the mystery of prayer. This book will become a classic."

Dr. R. T. Kendall, minister of Westminster
Chapel (1977–2002)

"There is probably no more important topic for the day we live in than why and how God answers prayer. Michael Youssef's *Life-Changing Prayers* will create both inspiration and faith to find out for yourself just how great our God is!"

Jim Cymbala

To John and Cindy Morris
in deep appreciation
for your faithful friendship and partnership
in the gospel of Jesus

# Contents

# Introduction

## *Counting Stars When We Can See None*

Have you ever wondered, *Has God abandoned me? Does He still keep His promises?*

Have you ever asked yourself, *What is God's plan for my life?* or *What is His plan for my children?*

Have you ever pleaded with God in prayer, then wondered, *Why doesn't He answer? Why does He delay, month after month, year after year?*

Have you ever thought, *Is it a sin to feel that God has let me down and forgotten me? Should I continue to trust Him?*

Have you ever tried to do God's will in your own way—with disastrous results? Have you ever tried to get ahead of God's will and speed up His timetable?

Have you ever wanted a child of your own so badly that you would do anything—anything!—to make it happen, yet the door to parenthood was slammed in your face and bolted shut?

If you can identify with any of these feelings and experiences, then the story of Abraham speaks to you. History changes, culture changes, technology changes, but human nature hasn't changed since the human race began. We are all the same under the skin. The story of Abraham is your story and mine.

What do you have in common with Abraham, this Old Testament man of faith? Not much, right? After all, Abraham lived four thousand years ago amid strange cultures and customs in a distant region of the world.

What does a man of his era have to say to people who use the internet and smartphones, who struggle with income taxes and credit card debt, who work in office buildings and get stuck in traffic, who worry about terrorism and nuclear war and the international debt crisis? What does a man of Abraham's era have to say to us in the twenty-first century?

And yet, as we study the story of Abraham and his wife Sarah, we find that Abraham's life speaks to us in surprising ways. In fact, the closer we look at Abraham, the more we realize that, in every way that truly matters, he's just like you and me. His story is the story of your journey of faith and mine.

Abraham was a man of faith, and we can learn how to live a life of faith by studying his story. He was a flawed man, just as you and I are flawed human beings. He sinned, he disobeyed, he tried to force God's hand and bend God's will—with disastrous results. Yet despite Abraham's sins and imperfections, he was called "the friend of God."

The pivotal moment in the story of Abraham—and the key insight for our lives—is found in Genesis 15:5. There, God takes Abraham outside at night and shows him the heavens. "Look up at the sky and count the stars—if indeed you can count them. . . . So shall your offspring be."

When God called Abraham out of Ur of the Chaldeans and promised to make of him a great nation, Abraham was seventy years old, his wife was sixty, and they were childless. When Abraham left Harran for the promised land, he was seventy-five. Ten years later, when Abraham was eighty-five, God renewed His promise to Abraham and told him that his offspring would be as numerous as the stars in the night sky. God invited Abraham to count the stars, and those stars not only symbolized Abraham's descendants—they were also emblems of God's promises and Abraham's faith.

In years to come, Abraham would go through times of darkness, times when there were no stars to be seen. He would wonder, *Has God abandoned me? Will He still keep His promise? What is His plan for my life—and for my children? Why doesn't He answer my prayer? Why does He delay?*

Yet Abraham would not give up on God, even though he had to wait for thirty years—past his hundredth birthday— for God to give him a son, the first of those "stars" God had promised him.

Despite his discouragement and the dreariness of those childless years, despite the mocking and derision of his neighbors, Abraham continued to look skyward. He continued to count stars—*even when there were no stars to be seen.*

In these pages, you will discover the rich life principles of Abraham's story. You'll learn to count God's promises to you—the many promises He has given you in His Word. God has made more than three thousand promises to us in the Bible—promises of:

11

Abundant life

Answers to our questions

Assurance for our doubts

Blessings for our lives and our families

Comfort in our sorrows

Compassion for our sufferings

Confidence for our challenges

Courage for dangerous times

Defense from our enemies

Deliverance from temptation

Direction for the journey

Encouragement for our weariness

Everlasting life

Faith for the future

Forgiveness for the past

Freedom from worry and anxiety

Friendship with God

Grace for each day

Guidance for our plans

Healing for our diseases

Help in times of trouble

Hope in times of despair

Inheritance that will never fade

Joy in times of sorrow

Justice when we have been wronged

Love that never fails

Mercy that never runs out

Peace that passes understanding
Pleasures everlasting
Power for any problem
Presence of God
Protection from perils
Provision for our needs
Refuge in times of trouble
Renewal of fading strength
Rescue when we call for help
Rest and restoration for our souls
Rewards for obedient service
Salvation by grace through faith
Satisfaction that is soul deep
Shelter in the time of storm
Success for the plans He gives us
Victory over obstacles and opposition
Vindication before accusers
Wisdom when we call upon Him

These are just a few of the promises He makes to us. These are the promises God has given us in His Word. These are the stars God has given us to count.

God told Abraham to count the stars even when he could see no stars. And God tells you and me to count the stars of His promises—even when the night is black and starless, even when our circumstances close in like a specter from a nightmare.

As we walk alongside Abraham through the journey of his life and faith, we will see his trust in God fail from time to time, just as we so easily falter in our own faith. But we will also see Abraham learning and growing in faith and obedience. We will see God patiently lifting him up, brushing him off, and setting him on his feet again. And we will learn how to keep moving onward and upward with God, how to keep counting stars when we can see none.

What are the stars God is telling you to count today? You may not be able to see those stars in the darkness of your circumstances, but like Abraham, you can count them with eyes of faith.

Let Abraham's testimony be yours as well. His faith was not in vain, and neither is yours. As Hebrews 11:12 testifies, "From this one man, and he as good as dead, came descendants as numerous as the stars in the sky and as countless as the sand on the seashore."

What do we have in common with this Old Testament man of faith? Everything! Join me as we step four thousand years back in time and find a flesh-and-blood human being just like you and me—failing, growing, and showing us how we too, even in the dark times of life, can count the stars of God's unfailing promises.

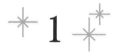

# 1

# Seven Promises

Have you ever tried to count the stars?

The Greek-Roman astronomer Ptolemy, who lived in Alexandria, Egypt, in the second century AD, was the first scientist to catalog the visible stars in the night sky. His book, the *Almagest*, charts the location of 1,022 stars—all the stars Ptolemy could see.

About fourteen hundred years after Ptolemy, Danish astronomer Tycho Brahe discovered an error in Ptolemy's *Almagest*, and he decided to make a new and more accurate catalog of the stars. Tycho was a walking paradox—a scientist with a disciplined, logical mind who was also known for his emotional extremes. As a university student, he became enraged over a remark his cousin had made, and they fought a sword duel in the dark. The cousin struck a blow that creased Tycho's forehead and lopped off his nose—and Tycho wore a nose made of brass for the rest of his life.

Tycho began journaling his nightly observations of the stars in 1563. The telescope had not been invented yet, but he used the most accurate measuring devices of his era to chart the precise location of every visible star. He completed his catalog of a thousand stars in 1597, thirty-four years after he began.[1] Imagine the dedication of Tycho Brahe, devoting nearly three and a half decades of his life to one task—counting the stars of the sky and charting their positions.

In Genesis 15, God uses the image of counting stars as an analogy for faith in His promises. God tells Abraham to count the stars—and He promises that Abraham's descendants will be as numerous as the stars in the heavens. At that point in his life, Abraham was in his eighties and had no children. Yet God had promised him descendants, and Abraham believed God's promise.

As you look closely at Abraham's journey of faith, you see that it was not all smooth sailing. Abraham faced many challenges in his journey with God. He experienced doubt and fear. He battled his own inner demons. He went left when God told him to go right. He failed and he sinned. He was often tempted to give up his faith in God, yet God said, "Keep counting stars, Abraham! Keep trusting in My promises."

The reason Abraham is the central figure in the Old Testament is because he persevered in his faith. He kept counting stars regardless of his circumstances. All Abraham had to go on were God's words spoken into his own heart. Abraham didn't have the Bible. He didn't have a pastor or a Bible study group or a Christian website to help him understand God's words. All he had were the words of almighty God, spoken directly to him, saying, "I know you have no stars right now but start counting stars anyway."

The night God first took Abraham out of his tent and showed him the night sky, the canopy of stars overhead became an abiding symbol of Abraham's trust in God. Those stars were the sparkling symbol of Abraham's shining faith in God until the day he drew his last breath.

## Stuck in Harran

The story of Abraham begins in the closing verses of Genesis 11. The name Abraham was given at birth was Abram, which means "Exalted Father" in the Hebrew language. God will change Abram's name to Abraham ("Father of a Multitude") when he is ninety-nine years old and receives the covenant of circumcision.[2] Throughout this book, to avoid confusion, I'll call him by his later name, Abraham.

He was born in the city of Ur of the Chaldeans on the south bank of the Euphrates River in lower Mesopotamia, the land now known as Iraq. His father was Terah and his brothers were Nahor and Haran (the father of Lot). Joshua 24:2 tells us, "Terah . . . lived beyond the Euphrates River and worshiped other gods." Abraham's wife was named Sarai (she will later be called Sarah), and she was unable to conceive a child.

In Genesis 12, God tells Abraham:

Go from your country, your people and your father's household to the land I will show you.

> I will make you into a great nation,
>     and I will bless you;
> I will make your name great,
>     and you will be a blessing.
> I will bless those who bless you,
>     and whoever curses you I will curse;

17

and all peoples on earth
    will be blessed through you. (vv. 1–3)

So Abraham, his wife Sarai, his father, Terah, and his nephew Lot set off for Canaan—but something happens along the way. They stop in the Assyrian city of Harran in upper Mesopotamia. Today, you can visit the ruins of Harran, located near the village of Altınbaşak in southern Turkey. In Abraham's day, Harran was a bustling and wealthy city, a site of religious, cultural, and commercial activity. Though God had called Abraham to the land of Canaan, he and his family stop and settle in Harran.

The Bible doesn't tell us why they settled there, but the reason is not hard to guess: Harran is a worldly, exciting city, the ancient world's version of Las Vegas. It probably wasn't Abraham who chose to settle in Harran; that was almost certainly Terah's decision. Abraham's father, a man who "worshiped other gods," was enticed by the worldliness, the people, and the nightlife in Harran. It was a city filled with temples and altars to many false gods. Abraham didn't agree with his father, but he respected his father's wishes. So, even though God had called Abraham to the land of Canaan, Terah and all his family settled in Harran.

Abraham and Sarai would remain stuck in Harran until Terah died.

## A Place of Compromise and Confusion

The life of Abraham is a mirror for your life and mine.

Like Abraham, every believer, every follower of the Lord Jesus Christ, has been called by God to come out of the old country of sin and go to a new land, a promised land. We were all born in the country of sin. We were born with our backs turned toward God. We were born in a state of rebellion, with hearts that were indifferent and hostile to God. Our pre-Christian lives were our Ur of the Chaldeans.

God called to us and said, "Come and follow Me. Leave your life of sin, turn away from your old ways. Let go of your selfishness and stubbornness and rebellion, your confusion and lostness, and start walking in the way I will show you. I will forgive your sins because of the shed blood of My Son, Jesus Christ. I will heal your wounded spirit and your wounded soul. I will give you a new identity. I will give you a heart that desires obedience to Me. I will adopt you as My child, and you will become an inheritor of all that belongs to Jesus. That is My promise to you, more certain and reliable than the stars in the sky. From now on, I want you to count the stars, because the blessings I will shower upon your life will be more numerous than the stars in the heavens."

When you made a decision for Christ, and you passed from death to everlasting life, from condemnation to forgiveness, that is the message God spoke into your life. You may not have heard that message in those words. You may not have understood what God was saying to you. But that was His message to you as He welcomed you into His forever family.

Perhaps you began your new life in Christ with a sense of joy and excitement. You may have thought, *What a thrill it is to know Jesus! What an adventure it is to belong to Him!* And you began counting the stars of blessing God was showering on your life. He had called you out of Ur and pointed your feet toward the promised land, toward Canaan. You were thrilled to be on your new journey with God.

But along the way, something happened—the same thing that happened to Abraham. After surrendering your life to Jesus and experiencing the joy of knowing Him, the excitement wore off. You found yourself bogged down in the middle of your journey. You found yourself in Harran.

What is Harran? It's a spiritual Las Vegas. It is a place of compromise and confusion and sin. It's a place of spiritual impediments and roadblocks, a place where you lose your joy and your will to move forward with God. It's a place of stagnation, a place where your spiritual journey comes to a standstill.

God saved you out of Ur so that you could live the victorious life in Canaan. He blessed you with all the rich blessings of Canaan. As the apostle Paul tells us, God's will is that you would continually grow and change "from glory to glory," with each new day becoming more and more like Christ.[3]

Yet here you are, stuck in Harran, stranded in a spiritual Las Vegas.

You began well when you said yes to Jesus. But before long, you began to mix the old with the new. Compromise set in. You began to settle for the mediocrity of a half-hearted faith.

How do you escape from Harran? How do you escape the clutches of your spiritual Las Vegas and get back on the road to Canaan? How do you get out of the ditch and get back on that higher plane of faith and glory?

## Don't Compromise with the World

When God called Abraham, he was steeped in the worship of false gods. Idolatry had sunk its claws deep into the soul and flesh of Abraham's family. Many Christians assume that the people whose stories are told in the Bible were super-saints. Not true! They were flesh-and-blood people who failed and sinned, just as you and I do. This is certainly true of Abraham and his family.

In Genesis 29–31, we find the story of Abraham's grandson Jacob and his marriage to Leah and to Rachel, the two daughters of Laban, Abraham's great-nephew. Laban had tricked Jacob into working for him for fourteen years as a dowry for Rachel. Later, he coaxed Jacob into working six more years after the fourteen years had ended. Finally, Jacob decided he'd had enough, and he took his wives, his servants, and his possessions and fled.

Before Rachel joined Jacob, she went into Laban's tent and stole her father's idols—his false gods.[4] The Bible doesn't tell us why she stole the idols. Perhaps Rachel was an idolater herself and thought the idols would bring her good luck. But this scene shows that the sin of idolatry was embedded deeply in Abraham's family. There is nothing more offensive to God than when His children, whom He has redeemed and saved, begin to mix false religion with the truth, the old way of life with the new life.

In Revelation 3 the Lord addresses the church in the city of Laodicea, and He condemns that church for having one foot in the world and one foot in the Christian faith. "I know your deeds," He says, "that you are neither cold nor hot. I wish you were either one or the other! So, because you are lukewarm—neither hot nor cold—I am about to spit you out of my mouth" (vv. 15–16).

That kind of lukewarm spirituality was what Abraham lived out in Harran. Halfway between Ur and Canaan, Abraham had reached a point of halfway obedience to God—and there he stayed. God had to get Abraham out of Harran, because He is a jealous God. He won't share His children with the world, and He won't leave His children in a land of half-hearted faith.

Some believers compromise their faith because they want to be accepted by the world. They don't want to be hated and mocked for their obedience to Christ. They don't want to be accused of being sexist and waging a "war against women" for opposing abortion. They don't want to be accused of being bigoted and homophobic for taking a stand for the biblical definition of marriage.

It's a lie of Satan that Christians are unloving and prejudiced and don't believe in equality. We should not be surprised that the world hates us. Jesus said that the world would hate us because the world hated Him.[5] As Christians, we love homosexual people with the love of Christ, even though we do not support their behavior or same-sex marriage. Yet I've known pastors who were so desperate to avoid being called antigay that they sacrificed biblical truth on the altar of being accepted by the world. They compromised their faith and settled in Harran.

The world hates our righteousness, our biblical standards, and our gospel message. We should expect to be hated and persecuted, and we should not let the hatred of the world keep us from obeying the Lord. When we obey God, we follow the example of Noah. Hebrews 11 tells us, "By faith Noah, when warned about things not yet seen, in holy fear built an ark to save his family. By his faith he condemned the world and became heir of the righteousness that is in keeping with faith" (v. 7).

Noah didn't set out to deliberately condemn the world by living faithfully and obediently before God. He wanted to save the world and invite as many people as possible to join him and his family in the ark. But when his neighbors saw his faith and his obedience, they felt condemned. Their own sinfulness and guilt condemned them.

We don't even have to open our mouths to convict the people around us of their sin. Our obedient and moral way of life will enrage those who rebel against God. Don't be surprised by their vindictive hate. Instead, rejoice in their false accusations. That's right, rejoice! That's what Jesus tells us in the Beatitudes: "Blessed are you when people insult you, persecute you and falsely say all kinds of evil against you because of me. Rejoice and be glad, because great is your reward in heaven, for in the same way they persecuted the prophets who were before you" (Matt. 5:11–12).

## A Sevenfold Promise: "I Will"

After Abraham's father died, Abraham continued on the journey. Abraham had to leave his past behind. He had to forsake all that had been near and dear to him in Ur. He had to move to a place he had never seen—a place that was strange and unknown to him.

Abraham's trek toward Canaan must have been a lonely journey. Yes, Sarai went with him, and his nephew Lot. But did they understand the strange calling God had given him? Did they understand that when Abraham heard a voice they couldn't hear, when he received a summoning they couldn't understand, Abraham was in direct contact with Yahweh, the maker of the universe? I doubt it. I think Abraham must

23

have felt totally alone with this calling God had spoken into his heart and soul.

But Abraham wasn't alone. God was with him, and God was all he truly needed.

You and I have a great privilege as Christians. We never have to walk alone in our Christian lives. God is with us. Our brothers and sisters in the church are with us. That is God's promise to us, just as it was His promise to Abraham—we are never alone.

In the first three verses of Genesis 12, God tells Abraham: I will show you a land. I will make you into a great nation. I will bless you. I will make your name great. I will bless those who bless you. I will curse those who curse you. God makes seven "I will" promises to Abraham. If you were keeping count, you may have noticed that I listed only six. That's because God gives Abraham the seventh promise later. God spoke the first six promises when Abraham still lived in Ur of the Chaldeans. He spoke the seventh promise to Abraham after Abraham left Harran and arrived in Canaan:

> So Abram went, as the LORD had told him; and Lot went with him. Abram was seventy-five years old when he set out from Harran. He took his wife Sarai, his nephew Lot, all the possessions they had accumulated and the people they had acquired in Harran, and they set out for the land of Canaan, and they arrived there.
>
> Abram traveled through the land as far as the site of the great tree of Moreh at Shechem. At that time the Canaanites were in the land. The LORD appeared to Abram and said, "To your offspring I will give this land." So he built an altar there to the LORD, who had appeared to him. (Gen. 12:4–7)

The seventh promise is, "To your offspring I will give this land," the land of Canaan. Implicit in all seven promises is God's promise to be present with Abraham. God promises His presence to everyone who repents of sin and turns to Him for forgiveness. We are His children, and He loves us with a strong, fatherly love.

It's instructive to notice the contrast between these seven wonderful "I will" promises of God and the five rebellious "I will" statements of Satan. In Isaiah 14, Satan says:

> I will ascend to the heavens;
> I will raise my throne
>   above the stars of God;
> I will sit enthroned on the mount of assembly,
>   on the utmost heights of Mount Zaphon.
> I will ascend above the tops of the clouds;
>   I will make myself like the Most High. (vv. 13–14)

Because of Satan's rebellious boasting, God expelled Satan from heaven. God's "I will" statements are promises of love. Satan's "I will" statements are boasts of hate.

When God makes His seven "I will" promises in Genesis 12, all He asks Abraham to do in return is to walk away from his past, with its idols and sin, and go to a new land that God will show him. If Abraham will do that, God will shower these sevenfold blessings on Abraham's life. Whenever God says "I will" and we respond to His promise, He blesses us.

There is a natural progression to the promises God makes to Abraham. They progress from one glory to the next. The Christian life is not a static, motionless state of being. God didn't design this life to be a waiting room. He designed the Christian life to be a journey, a progression, an adventure.

At times, it seems like an obstacle course. But as we go, we grow, and we move from glory to glory. You can see the progression from one glory to the next in the seven promises God makes to Abraham.

### Promise #1: I Will Show You a Land

God's first promise to Abraham is "I will show you a land." God's seventh and last promise to Abraham is "I will give you a land." Abraham goes from seeing to receiving. First, God will show him the land; ultimately, Abraham will possess it. His total trust in God is the key to receiving the promises of God.

In the same way, God says to us, "I'm going to show you the great blessings in store for you as you walk with Me and serve Me if you keep Me foremost in your life." And a day will come when we reach the land He has promised, and we will possess that land and will rule and reign with Him forever.

But we must choose to walk with Him to the land He has shown us. We must choose to trust Him, obey Him, and go where He leads. Whenever I choose to go my own way, I get clobbered, I end up defeated, I lose my way. But whenever I go where He chooses, I am totally blessed. You can probably testify to that same truth in your own life.

God has given us the gift of free will, and we can use it to choose His way or to go our own way. Be careful about the choices you make. Yes, you can choose to go your own way—to settle in Harran after God has called you to Canaan. And God will let you have your own way—at least for a time. But you will find that when you do so, you nullify God's promise to you. When you go your own way, you'll find there is no blessing at the end of the path.

But if you take His hand and go where He leads you, He will bless you in ways you can't begin to imagine.

### Promise #2: I Will Make You into a Great Nation

God's second promise to Abraham is that he will become a great nation. This is the first of many unconditional promises God made to Abraham. It's just as well that it was unconditional, because if it was conditioned upon Abraham's faithfulness and performance, and that of his descendants, the promise would have been null and void very quickly. Abraham failed God miserably, and so did his descendants.

Again and again in the Scriptures, we see that there are conditional promises and unconditional promises. Many Christians confuse the two. They claim God's conditional promises without meeting the conditions.

When God chose us in Christ, that was an act of sheer grace. It was unconditional. It had nothing to do with us. We were lost in sin and incapable of meeting the demands of a just and holy God. Our salvation was a gift of His grace, not based on our works. We had nothing to do with our salvation except the decision to receive it. But now that we are saved, we find that there are a number of conditional promises in our Christian walk.

This is important to notice: When God made this unconditional promise to Abraham—"I will make you into a great nation"—Abraham was seventy years old and Sarah was sixty. When God told Abraham to start counting stars, he was past retirement age. He was drawing Social Security, he had joined AARP, and he and Sarah qualified for the senior discount at Waffle House. It is impossible to comprehend the kind of faith it takes for a childless man of Abraham's advanced years to believe God's promise that He will make of Abraham a great nation.

Yet Abraham took God at His word and counted stars, even though he could see no stars. That is genuine faith in the pure biblical sense.

"But Lord, I'm old!" *Start counting stars, Abraham.*

"What if I wander away from Your will?" *Keep counting stars, Abraham.*

"But Lord, what if my descendants fall away from You?" *Keep counting stars, Abraham.*

"What if they become idol worshipers? What if they worship Baal and Molech?" *Keep counting stars, Abraham.*

Why could God make an unconditional promise to Abraham that He would make of Abraham a great nation? Because the greatness of that nation didn't depend on the faithfulness of Abraham or his descendants. God's unconditional promise to Abraham was not fulfilled by Abraham or his offspring. God's unconditional promise was fulfilled by "the seed" of Abraham. Who or what is "the seed" of Abraham?

The apostle Paul answers this question in his Letter to the Galatians: "The promises were spoken to Abraham and to his seed. Scripture does not say 'and to seeds,' meaning many people, but 'and to your seed,' meaning one person, who is Christ" (Gal. 3:16; see Gen. 12:7; 13:15; 24:7). For centuries, Jewish scholars and teachers misunderstood what God's promise meant. They interpreted *seed* in a plural-collective sense, never realizing that God was using *seed* in a singular sense, meaning not many seeds but the one seed—Jesus the Messiah.

Millions of people around the world today and billions down through history have worshiped the living God because of the blessings He showered on Abraham, blessings that are fulfilled in Jesus. As Paul writes in Galatians 3:

> So also Abraham "believed God, and it was credited to him as righteousness."
>
> Understand, then, that those who have faith are children of Abraham. Scripture foresaw that God would justify the Gentiles by faith, and announced the gospel in advance to Abraham: "All nations will be blessed through you." So those who rely on faith are blessed along with Abraham, the man of faith. (vv. 6–9)

It's no wonder that when Jesus said, "Before Abraham was born, I am," the religious leaders picked up stones and wanted to kill Him.[6] They thought they were the seeds of Abraham, his promised descendants. But it was Jesus who was *the* seed, and through Him, countless people from every nation around the world would come to a saving faith and eternal life. And Jesus, the singular seed of Abraham, was also the preexistent and eternal Creator.[7]

### Promise #3: I Will Bless You

Abraham didn't ask God to bless him, but God graciously promised that He would bless Abraham's life. God would bless Abraham in ways he could never imagine, much less expect.

Please understand, there is nothing wrong with asking God to bless you, nothing whatsoever. But I don't believe

29

you need to ask. God has promised to bless you when you follow Him by faith and go where He sends you.

I can testify to the fact that over the past few decades, God has richly blessed me in ways I have never dared or thought to ask. In saying that, I'm not bragging about myself, because I fail Him all the time. But God knows that in my own fallible and failure-prone way, I seek to serve His kingdom with all my heart. I seek to glorify King Jesus. And to my utter amazement, God blesses me beyond anything I would think to ask. I do not expect God's blessing, I do not deserve God's blessing, I do not ask for God's blessing, but I receive His gracious blessing. That is how our loving God works.

I ask God to bless the ministry He has built in our church and in our global ministry, Leading The Way. I ask Him to bless His message as I teach and preach and write. I spend my time praying for others and praying for the kingdom of God, then seeking first His kingdom every waking moment.

And God, by His grace, blesses me beyond measure.

### Promise #4: I Will Make Your Name Great

God tells Abraham, "I will make your name great, and you will be a blessing" (Gen. 12:2). For four thousand years, Jews have claimed Abraham as their father. Christians have claimed Abraham as their father for two thousand years. Even Muslims, who adhere to a works-based religion out of fear rather than faith, have looked to Abraham as their father for fourteen hundred years.

What does the name of Abraham stand for? It stands for immovable faith and trust in the living God. The name stands for what God has promised. The name stands for what God has done. The name stands for God's faithfulness.

Abraham's original name, Abram, meant only "Exalted Father." But God changed his name from Abram to Abraham, "Father of a Multitude." This symbolized the fact that Abraham's faith in the one true God would one day be shared by multitudes of people from every tribe and language and nation. Abraham's descendants are Jews and Europeans, North Americans and South Americans, Black Africans and Arabs, Asians and Pacific Islanders.

Galatians 3:14 tells us, "He redeemed us in order that the blessing given to Abraham might come to the Gentiles through Christ Jesus, so that by faith we might receive the promise of the Spirit." Abraham's greatest descendant by far is the Lord Jesus Christ. The world is blessed by coming to Jesus, the seed of Abraham. People all around the world are saved and redeemed and rejoicing, even in the midst of persecution, because of that one descendant of Abraham, the Lord Jesus Christ.

### Promises #5 and #6: Blessings—and Cursings

God promises Abraham, "I will bless those who bless you, and whoever curses you I will curse; and all peoples on earth will be blessed through you" (Gen. 12:3). Through the ages of history, God has made good on that promise countless times.

When Joseph, the great-grandson of Abraham, was sold into slavery in Egypt, the Bible said that God blessed Egypt because of Joseph. When Rahab the prostitute aided the spies who came into Jericho, God blessed Rahab and her family for blessing the nation of Israel. There are many other examples I could cite.

I believe that one reason God has richly blessed America is because America has taken the gospel to the ends of the earth and has blessed many nations, especially Israel.

As a Christian, you don't go out of your way to make enemies. You don't try to antagonize people into cursing you. But if you stand up for your faith, if you simply say, "I'm a follower of Jesus Christ," you will instantly have enemies. If you don't make enemies, you are probably not taking a bold enough stand for your faith.

There is no one I hate or hold a grudge against. No matter what other people may do to me, from my perspective, they are not my enemy. They may see me as an enemy, they may hate me, they may wish me harm, but I will not hate them back. God has promised to fight our battles for us. If anyone curses us, God will be our shield, our defender, and, if necessary, our avenger. He will deal with anyone who curses us, and He will be more just and thorough than you or I could ever be.

I once had a conversation with an angry young man. He was bitter because of some injustice that was done to him. He wanted to take matters into his own hands. I told him, "The blessing I have of having lived a few years longer than you is that I have seen the Lord take care of these matters for me. I've seen God do a much better job of avenging wrongs than I could ever do. So be patient. Trust God. Leave this matter in His hands."

Sure enough, a few weeks later, God took care of the problem for this young man. God always proves His faithfulness, and He always keeps His promises.

## *Promise #7: I Will Give This Land to Your Offspring*

When God said, "To your offspring I will give this land," Abraham had no offspring and no land. He was counting stars when he could see none. Not only that, but Abraham and Sarah died in the land of promise without owning any land. More than four hundred years later, God fulfilled His promise to Abraham. Following the death of Moses, under the leadership of Joshua, the descendants of Abraham marched into Canaan and took possession of the land of promise.

God fulfills His promises to the third and fourth and tenth and hundredth generations. His promises are more real than the book you are holding in your hands. The same can be said for the promises that Jesus made to His followers in the New Testament, such as, "Come to me, all you who are weary and burdened, and I will give you rest. Take my yoke upon you and learn from me, for I am gentle and humble in heart, and you will find rest for your souls" (Matt. 11:28–29).

You may be carrying the weight of a refrigerator on your back, feeling so weary you can't take another step. Go to Jesus, tell Him about your burdens and sorrows, and He will take that weight off your back and load it onto Himself. He has already taken your heaviest burden—your sins—onto Himself at the cross.

The story of Jesus and the rich young ruler is told in Matthew 19, Mark 10, and Luke 18. A rich young man asked Jesus how to attain eternal life. Jesus told the young man to obey the commandments. The young man responded that he already did so. What else should he do? Jesus replied, "If you want to be perfect, go, sell your possessions and give to the poor, and you will have treasure in heaven. Then come, follow me" (Matt. 19:21).

In other words, Jesus tells him, "Give up your idols—the wealth and possessions that actually possess you—and be my disciple. Then you will have treasures in heaven." But the rich young man couldn't let go of his idols, so he went away, sorrowing.

To follow Jesus, we have to leave our old country behind and go to the promised land as God commanded. Like Abraham, we must go to the land we cannot see, the land God has promised to us, the land He will show us.

Have you heard God calling you to the promised land? Have you taken the first step? Or are you still in Ur? Or maybe you started out for the promised land, but you're stranded in Harran. What is keeping you from going all the way to the promised land with God?

If you have never taken that first step of faith, if you have never confessed your sins to God and asked Him to forgive you through the blood of Jesus, you can do so today, right now, before you turn another page of this book. You can be eternally saved and be blessed with the presence of God. You can be filled with the person and power of the Holy Spirit.

You know where you stand with God. If you have heard the voice of the Holy Spirit, if He has spoken to you through His Word, don't wait another moment. Respond now.

# 2

# A Pilgrim—or a Drifter?

John Bunyan wrote his allegorical novel *The Pilgrim's Progress* while serving time in the Bedfordshire county prison. His crime: preaching the gospel without a license. It was against the law to hold church services that were not authorized by the established state church, the Church of England. *The Pilgrim's Progress* has remained continuously in print since it was first published in 1678, and it has been translated into more than two hundred languages. I first read it when I was a twelve-year-old boy in Egypt.

The book tells the story of a Christian named Pilgrim who progresses through life on his journey to heaven, his ultimate destination. Throughout his journey, he encounters many perils, challenges, and temptations, just as we do today. He also finds places of rest, as God provides for us as well.

At one point, Pilgrim finds himself in a city called Vanity Fair. William Makepeace Thackeray wrote a novel by that title about Victorian English society, and an American magazine called *Vanity Fair* deals with fashion and culture; both are named after this scene in *Pilgrim's Progress*. Vanity Fair is a city that was built by the demon Beelzebub. All the things human beings desire and lust after are sold every day in the marketplace of Vanity Fair: "houses, lands, trades, places, honours, preferments, titles, countries, kingdoms, lusts, pleasures, and delights of all sorts, as whores, bawds, wives, husbands, children, masters, servants, lives, blood, bodies, souls, silver, gold, pearls, precious stones, and what not."[1]

Bunyan tells us that there are three characteristics that distinguish Christians like Pilgrim from the worldly people of Vanity Fair. First, Christian pilgrims dress in clothing that is different from the people of Vanity Fair. The appearance of Christian pilgrims seems strange to the citizens of that worldly city. Second, Christians speak a different language, "the language of Canaan,"[2] the language of the promised land. That is not the local language of Vanity Fair. Third, Christians have different values from the people of Vanity Fair, and they show no interest in the materialism and pleasure seeking that is the stock-in-trade of Vanity Fair. Why are Christians different from the worldly people of Vanity Fair? The difference in clothing speaks of the fact that Christians wear a robe of righteousness, which Jesus gives to all believers and which the people of Vanity Fair don't have. The robe of righteousness, which was purchased by the blood of Jesus, makes the unrighteous people of Vanity Fair bitter and angry.

The language Christians speak is the language of God, yet the communication problem is not caused merely by a difference in language. Christians don't even talk about the same matters as the citizens of Vanity Fair. Christians speak about spiritual concerns, about matters that are near and dear to the heart of God. The people of Vanity Fair speak only of worldly things, from a worldly perspective.

The values of Pilgrim and other Christians are completely alien to the values of the people of this world, whose god is Satan and who are only interested in gratifying and elevating the self. If only twenty-first-century Christians would be as distinct from the world as the Christian pilgrims of *The Pilgrim's Progress*.

## Bound for Canaan

Hebrews 11 tells us that Abraham and Sarah and the other Old Testament heroes of the faith were "strangers and pilgrims on the earth."[3] What is a pilgrim?

It's important to have a precise definition in mind. A pilgrim is not just a person who leaves home and wanders around aimlessly; a pilgrim is not a drifter. A pilgrim is a person who travels with a destination clearly in mind. A pilgrim has a vision to accomplish, a goal to reach, a planned destination. A pilgrim is determined to reach his destination regardless of difficulties, obstacles, or suffering. Because of this vision, because of this goal, because of this determination, a pilgrim holds everything else in life—possessions, earthly ambitions, and even people—with open hands.

There are few things more heartbreaking than watching a spiritual pilgrim become a worldly drifter. There are few things more tragic than seeing someone who showed so much promise as a Christian, someone who was walking with God out of Ur and toward Canaan, get lost along the journey. I've known people who started out as pilgrims and became drifters, and my heart breaks for them.

At this crucial time in human history, God is looking for authentic, sincere pilgrims who will walk through the midst of this Vanity Fair world without being corrupted by it. Regardless of our age or our station in life, God is calling us to be His pilgrims in this troubled and sin-ridden world. That is what God teaches us through the life of this pilgrim named Abraham.

Genesis 12 tells us how Abram (that is, Abraham) and his wife Sarai departed from Harran, bound for Canaan. The Bible does not waste words. It's important to notice the details in this account:

> So Abram went, as the LORD had told him; and Lot went with him. Abram was seventy-five years old when he set out from Harran. He took his wife Sarai, his nephew Lot, all the possessions they had accumulated and the people they had acquired in Harran, and they set out for the land of Canaan, and they arrived there. (vv. 4–5)

When Abraham left Harran, he took with him a great deal of accumulated wealth. At this time, Abraham was 75 years old. For a man who would live to be 175, this was middle age. The possessions Abraham had acquired during his stay in Harran did not stop him from being a genuine follower of God. Wealth is a trap for many believers. But in the hands of a wise and generous disciple of the Lord, wealth is a source of blessing and ministry. In my almost-fifty years of ministry, I've known a number of people who have been materially blessed by God but who have never made an idol of wealth.

They used their wealth to serve God and others. Abraham was that kind of disciple.

Abraham, Sarah, Terah, and Lot had traveled a distance of seven hundred miles, traveling north by northeast, to get from Ur to Harran. After living in Harran for five years or so, Abraham's father, Terah, died. After burying his father, Abraham resumed his pilgrimage down to Canaan, a distance of another seven hundred miles or so, traveling south by southeast.

I want to look at this Old Testament account in light of a New Testament passage, Acts 7. There Stephen, the first Christian martyr, stands before the Sanhedrin, the ruling council in Jerusalem. This is the same ruling council that condemned Jesus to death and that later also persecuted Peter and John. Stephen knows the murderous hearts of the Sanhedrin members, yet he fearlessly bears witness to what God is doing through Jesus and His church. Stephen is showing how God is at work among the people despite the efforts of these rulers to oppose God. Stephen says:

> Brothers and fathers, listen to me! The God of glory appeared to our father Abraham while he was still in Mesopotamia, before he lived in Harran. "Leave your country and your people," God said, "and go to the land I will show you."
>
> So he left the land of the Chaldeans and settled in Harran. After the death of his father, God sent him to this land where you are now living. (vv. 2–4)

Stephen says that Abraham settled in Harran. What kind of place was Harran? It was very much like the city of Vanity Fair, a place of temptations and enticements.

Notice Stephen's phrase, "after the death of his father." These six words speak volumes. Again, the Bible does not waste words. Stephen is speaking before the Sanhedrin—a group of powerful Middle Eastern men. I want you to hear this story as they heard it, through the perspective of the Middle Eastern culture. I'm going to retell the story of Abraham and his father, Terah. Please understand, this is the Michael Youssef version of the story and does not have the authority of Scripture. I am merely using my "baptized imagination" to retell the story.

### Terah's "Apron Strings"

Picture with me the scene that takes place in Ur of the Chaldeans. God tells Abraham, "I want you to leave Ur. I want you to leave your present life behind and go to the land that I will show you."

So Abraham went to the tent of his father, Terah, opened the tent flap, and said, "Pops—!" Well, this being the Middle East, he would have probably said, "Abba!"

"What is it, Abram?"

"I have to leave Ur. I have to go away."

"Go? Where are you going, son?"

"I don't know where, Abba. I only know that God called it Canaan, and He's going to show me where to go."

"God? Which god? There are many gods. I have an entire shelf full of gods. Golden gods, silver gods, tin gods—"

"No, Abba. There's only one true God, and He is calling me to this far-off land called Canaan. I'm going to leave my hometown and go to this land—and Abba, I'm going to have to leave you."

Now, the part of the story I'm about to describe next is sheer speculation on my part; you won't find this in the Scriptures. But based on my knowledge of Middle Eastern culture, I think this may be what happened next. I think that when Terah heard his son Abram say that he was leaving Ur, this Middle Eastern father probably freaked out.

"What?" Terah said. "Abram, my son, I can't believe I heard you correctly! You're going to leave your poor father in Ur and take off for parts unknown? You would leave your old man, the father who's been good to you all these years? Who will take care of me in my old age? Abram, son, don't you love me?"

"Well, sure, I love you, Abba. But God said—"

"'God said!' Since when do the gods talk to us? My gods have never spoken to me!"

"But the one true God speaks, and He has told me to go to Canaan. He told me He is going to make a great nation of me."

"Abram, you can't leave Ur without me. If you're going to Canaan, I'm going too."

Middle Eastern families are very tightly bonded. Often, when a child wants to leave home and go far away, the parents take it as an insult. Abram loved and respected his father, Terah. He honored his father to the point where his obedience to God's call was hindered. Terah accompanied Abram and Sarai, and when they reached Harran, they stopped and settled. And there they stayed until Terah died and Abram was free to continue his pilgrimage to Canaan.

If you are a parent, I have a word of biblical counsel for you: when your children reach the age at which they should be out on their own, cut the apron strings. Give them their independence. And if you have the kind of child who wants to be dependent, who is content to live in your basement and play video games day and night, then *force* that child to get out on his own. You are not doing your adult child any favors by keeping him or her dependent on you. Don't spoil your child or make your adult child feel guilty for leaving home. Say, "You know I'll always love you and support you, and you're always welcome to visit. I will always pray for you, but it's time for you to earn your own living and live your own life."

One reason God called Abraham to leave Ur was to get him out of that center of idol worship. God wanted to get Abraham away from bad companions and a bad environment. He wanted to take Abraham away from his old life and on to his new life in Canaan.

Abraham had an unbelieving father. As a Christian, you must always love and respect and honor your parents. If they are nonbelievers, you must pray for them and witness to them and set a good example for them.

But if it ever comes down to a choice between obeying your parents and obeying God, always do what God calls you to do.

### Get Out While You Can

Abraham told his father he was going to Canaan, and Terah said he was going too. Genesis 11:31 contains a fascinating detail: "Terah took his son Abram, his grandson Lot son of Haran, and his daughter-in-law Sarai, the wife of his son Abram, and together they set out from Ur of the Chaldeans to go to Canaan." Who did God call? Abram. But the Bible tells us that "Terah took his son Abram." If God called Abram, shouldn't Abram have taken Terah on the journey instead of the other way around? It seems that Terah, Abram's father, wasn't letting Abram go anywhere without him.

I don't know if you see the humor in this, but I find it hilarious. God called Abraham, but Terah had to take him. Abraham couldn't or wouldn't go on his own. Terah also took Abraham's nephew Lot and Abraham's wife Sarah. Together they set off from Ur of the Chaldeans, heading for Canaan.

Midway in their journey, they reached Harran—and they settled there. Why? I believe it's because Harran was home to the great temple of Sin, the god of the moon. Tamara M. Green, head of the Department of Classical and Oriental Studies at Hunter College of the City University of New York, writes, "The political prominence of Harran in the Assyrian period was due in large measure to its protecting deity, Sin, the god of the Moon, and giver of oracles, guardian of treaties whose eye sees and knows all."[4] The temple of Sin, Professor Green adds, was called *Ehulhul*, which is Sumerian for "Temple of Rejoicing."

Abraham's father, Terah, saw the pagan temple of the moon god and he thought he had died and gone to pagan heaven. He loved the moon worship in the city of Harran. For a moon worshiper like Terah, the city of Harran was like Mecca to Muslims, Salt Lake City to Mormons, and the Vatican to Roman Catholics. This was the place of all places, Terah's Shangri-La.

When Terah arrived in Harran, he looked around and said, "Whoopee! Abram, my boy, I'm so glad I came with you! Forget Canaan. Let's stay here! This place is a pagan Disneyland!"

"But Abba, God called me to Canaan!"

"Canaan is seven hundred miles away. Why travel so far? This place has to be better than Canaan. This is where all the fun is!"

They had come to Harran in the land of compromise. They had arrived at Vanity Fair. Abraham was in great spiritual danger in Harran. This place was filled with temptations to materialism and idolatry, which threatened to pollute his faith in God.

If you are in Harran right now, I urge you to get out while the getting is good. Get out while it's still possible. Get out while God's will for your life can still be found. Don't settle in Harran. Don't settle for less than God's best.

We are all prone to settle for worldly enticements that fall far short of God's perfect plan for our lives. I know. I have personally experienced at least two Harrans in my life. I get emotional just thinking about this passage of Scripture, because God rescued me and saved me from both of my Harran experiences. He reached my heart before it was too late.

My prayer for you as a reader of this book is that you will not settle for Harran. I pray you will heed this warning in the story of Abraham and will get out of Harran without delay. Get on your knees and say, "Lord, I'm sorry I compromised and settled for Harran. I'm sorry I wandered away from the path You had set for me. I'm sorry I stopped short of going on to Canaan with You. Lead me out of Harran, Lord, and I promise I will follow You."

I know without a shadow of doubt that God will rejoice over this prayer, and He will empower you to act on it. God loves it when His people move out of their comfort zone and plunge into the adventure of the Christian life. He loves it when we implicitly trust Him with all our hearts. He loves it when we get off our blessed assurance and dare great things for God. He loves it when we invest everything we are and everything we have in His kingdom. He loves it when we count stars we can't even see—stars of His promises, stars of His blessings, stars that are ours even though storm clouds may hide them from view.

When we count stars we can't even see, we are walking by faith and not by sight. The eyes of faith will keep us on the right track, following God's vision for our lives. When we follow our own human wisdom and worldly vision, we get stuck in Harran.

Whatever your Harran may be—and I suspect God is already bringing something to your mind, something that means Harran to you, something that makes you feel stuck, trapped, and unable to move on toward Canaan—whatever it may be, tell God right now that you want to leave Harran behind. You want to move on with Him. You want to get back on the road and continue your pilgrimage with the Lord. Tell God you are ready to move *right now*—then take the first step, whatever that step may be.

Don't settle for Harran. Get out while you can. Don't wait till tomorrow or some other time. *Leave now.*


## Needed: An Invasion from Heaven

Next, we learn what Abraham did upon his arrival in the land of Canaan—and we learn what God said to Abraham:

> Abram traveled through the land as far as the site of the great tree of Moreh at Shechem. At that time the Canaanites

45

were in the land. The LORD appeared to Abram and said, "To your offspring I will give this land." So he built an altar there to the LORD, who had appeared to him.

From there he went on toward the hills east of Bethel and pitched his tent, with Bethel on the west and Ai on the east. There he built an altar to the LORD and called on the name of the LORD. (Gen. 12:6–8)

Abraham arrived in Canaan, and he found the land to be inhabited with Canaanites—fierce idol-worshiping tribes. Perhaps Abraham was troubled when he saw that the land to which God had called him was already occupied with unfriendly people. God appeared to Abraham and spoke to him, perhaps as a way of reassuring him. The Lord made a promise to Abraham: "To your offspring I will give this land." Relieved and rejoicing that God had reconfirmed His promise, Abraham built an altar to the Lord and called upon Him with praise and thanksgiving.

Do you want to see revival come to your church? Do you want revival in your community? In your nation? Then understand this: revival begins with you; revival begins with me. I'm not saying that we can, in our own strength, make revival happen. Only the Spirit of God can bring revival to a church or a nation. But revival happens when God's people invite Him in to take over their lives. Revival will come when each individual believer decides to move out of Harran and build an altar at Bethel.

Building an altar is a symbol that we are renewing our vision—God's vision—for our lives. That's what Abraham did when he got out of Harran and arrived in Canaan. He built an altar at Bethel, and he called on the name of the Lord.

Stephen Olford called revival "an invasion from heaven that brings a conscious awareness of God."[5] That holy invasion of our lives will not take place until we want God more than we want sin. David Wilkerson once said, "There are people having great emotional experiences right now and calling it revival. But I think true revival will come . . . [only when] people are driven to their knees to repent."[6] Revival will come when we run away from sin and run toward God, when we leave Harran and get back on the path to Canaan.

Abraham learned the hard way that personal revival will not be found in part-time or partial obedience. The secret is not in the destination but in the journey. The secret is not in the place we are going to but in the place of obedience, the place of holiness.

We don't hear that word *holiness* very much anymore, do we? But the Bible tells us that without holiness, no one can see God. The place of holiness is a place we reach when we ask God to examine our lives. As the psalmist writes:

> Search me, God, and know my heart;
> > test me and know my anxious thoughts.
> See if there is any offensive way in me,
> > and lead me in the way everlasting. (Ps.
> > 139:23–24)

No excuses, no finger-pointing, just honest, thorough examination of our heart and our conscience by God Himself: "Lord, examine my life. Open my heart for inspection. Is there sin in my life? Is there anything in my thoughts or speech or behavior that is offensive to you?"

Until we come clean with God as individual believers, acknowledging our disobedience and stubbornness, our desire for comfort and convenience and status and power, we will remain stuck in Harran. Until we admit to God and to ourselves that we have been doing our will, not God's will, going our way instead of His way, we will never move on to Canaan, we will never build an altar at Bethel, and we will never impact our culture for Christ.

I pray that the story of Abraham and his pilgrimage from Harran to Canaan would ignite a desire in your heart—a desire for revival, a desire to experience the reality of God in your life, a desire to enter the land God has promised to you.

## Another Great Awakening

J. Edwin Orr was a friend of mine and a great teacher of the Word of God. During the 1970s, I had the joy of being mentored by him. He was an authority on the awakenings and revivals that had taken place throughout the history of the church. He said that immediately after the Revolutionary War, the moral fiber and spiritual condition of America were in a tailspin. Alcoholism was rampant, crime was rising, and church attendance was declining. John Marshall, the chief justice of the United States Supreme Court at that time, wrote a letter to James Madison, the father of the Constitution, and said that the Christian church in America was "too far gone ever to be redeemed." And Thomas Paine, one of the intellectual leaders of the American Revolution, predicted, "Christianity will be forgotten in thirty years."[7]

A poll of the Harvard student body found that there was not a single student on the campus who believed in Jesus Christ. On the Princeton campus, the vast majority of students engaged in what they called the "filthy speech move-ment." At Williams College, students held a mock commu-nion that blasphemed the Lord Jesus. In New Jersey, students burned a Bible in a public bonfire. Crime was rampant, and women feared to go out on the public streets.[8]

In 1794, as the new American nation was sinking into god-lessness and depravity, a Connecticut preacher named Isaac Backus began holding prayer meetings at his church. Pastor Backus had been an influential minister during the Revolu-tionary War, and his 1778 book *Government and Liberty Described and Ecclesiastical Tyranny Exposed* was a major influence on the religious liberty clauses that the founding fathers wrote into the First Amendment to the Constitution. Backus also formed an alliance with twenty-four other New England ministers with a goal of praying regularly for a spiritual awakening throughout America. They called these prayer sessions "a concert of prayer."

By 1798, churches throughout the thirteen former colonies were holding prayer meetings, confessing sin, and pleading with God for revival. An amazing nationwide revival broke out across America, and especially on college campuses. This revival became known as the Second Great Awakening. As Dr. Orr once asked, "Is not this what is missing so much from all our evangelistic efforts: explicit agreement, visible unity, unusual prayer?"[9]

Change will happen when God's people repent of their sin and turn to Him. Revival starts with repentance, and repentance starts with us—not the outside world, not the government, not society, but us. When God's people repent of their sin and turn to Him and become fervent in prayer, then watch out! God is going to move among His people.

Take the first step. Get out of your Harran. Turn your steps toward Canaan. Count the stars of God's promises, even though you can see no stars. God is fulfilling the promises He made to Abraham—and He is fulfilling them in your life and mine today.

# 3

# A Failure of Faith

From Watergate to the Monica Lewinsky scandal to almost every other scandal involving public officials, we've seen that it's not the initial misdeed that usually leads to disgrace and downfall. The worst consequences, the deeper troubles, always seem to come from the cover-up.

The Bible exhorts us again and again that confession of sin brings healing, forgiveness, and God's restoration in our lives. Covering up sin, rationalizing sin, or blaming others only leads to deeper pain. As the psalmist writes:

> When I kept silent,
>     my bones wasted away
>     through my groaning all day long.
> For day and night
>     your hand was heavy on me;
> my strength was sapped
>     as in the heat of summer.
> Then I acknowledged my sin to you
>     and did not cover up my iniquity.

51

I said, "I will confess
  my transgressions to the LORD."
And you forgave
  the guilt of my sin. (Ps. 32:3–5)

There are few more powerful examples of this principle than the patriarch Abraham. So far, we have seen Abraham as essentially a paragon of faith and obedience, a friend of God who counted the stars of God's promises even when he could see none. Yes, he stayed longer than he should have in Harran—but he probably did so in deference and respect to his father, Terah. But as we are about to see, this hero of the faith did indeed have feet of clay. He was as prone to sin and deception as we are, and he would soon learn a very painful lesson about the consequences of lying and covering up sin.

## Those Who Go Down to Egypt

If I seem in the next few pages to be hard on Abraham, please know that's not my purpose. I identify with Abraham, including his faults and failings. He took some detours along the way to his destination in Canaan, and I have taken some spiritual detours as well. The concluding verses of Genesis 12 tell us what Abraham did after he built an altar to the Lord at Bethel:

Then Abram set out and continued toward the Negev.
  Now there was a famine in the land, and Abram went down to Egypt to live there for a while because the famine was severe. As he was about to enter Egypt, he said to his wife Sarai, "I know what a beautiful woman you are. When the Egyptians see you, they will say, 'This is his wife.' Then

52

they will kill me but will let you live. Say you are my sister, so that I will be treated well for your sake and my life will be spared because of you." (vv. 9–13)

Abram left Bethel and moved south, settling in the Negev. The Negev is the desert region that comprises the southern half of modern-day Israel. Perhaps Abraham worried that he would have trouble from his neighbors, the Canaanites. So he moved to a more sparsely populated part of the promised land.

When a famine overshadowed the land, Abraham took his wife and possessions and headed for Egypt. Throughout the Scriptures, Egypt symbolizes moving away from God. Egypt pictures for us our all-too-human tendency to trust in our own human ingenuity and resourcefulness instead of trusting in God. Egypt is synonymous with a lack of faith, with the error of walking by sight instead of walking by faith. The prophet Isaiah tells us:

> Woe to those who go down to Egypt for help,
>     who rely on horses,
> who trust in the multitude of their chariots
>     and in the great strength of their horsemen,
> but do not look to the Holy One of Israel,
>     or seek help from the LORD. (Isa. 31:1)

Isaiah is not speaking here of a geographical location in northeastern Africa. When he speaks of "Egypt," he is talking about an attitude of the heart. He is talking about those who turn for help to either a literal or metaphorical Egypt instead of turning to God. The only reason for turning to Egypt for help is a lack of faith in God.

## His Life—or His Wife?

In your life and mine, "going down to Egypt" can take many forms. It might mean placing our trust in a friend, only to find that our friend lets us down or deeply wounds us. Or it might mean placing our trust in our own strength and ingenuity, only to end up deeply disappointed with the choices we have made.

When famine came to the land, Abraham went down to Egypt instead of turning to God for help and sustenance. The moment he turned his steps toward Egypt, Abraham the pilgrim became Abraham the drifter. I can identify with Abraham. I have made the same spiritual error in my own life—more than once.

Your Egypt will be different from another person's Egypt. But the pattern will always be the same. Here's what happens when you develop a dependence on Egypt: whatever your Egypt may be, whether it's your net worth, your talents and skills, your reputation and standing in the community, your health and physical conditioning, or something else, you'll find that the moment you begin to place your faith and trust in Egypt, your intimacy with God will begin to die. You probably won't even notice it, but your affection toward God and your excitement in knowing Him will fade. Your love for Him will grow cold. Your relationship with Him will become formal and distant.

I remember that when I went into my metaphorical Egypt, I couldn't stand pastors during that time. I couldn't listen to the preaching of the Word. I rationalized these feelings of annoyance, and I blamed the preachers—but they weren't the problem. The problem was my own heart.

When we are in an Egypt state of mind, we begin to rationalize, blame others, and tell ourselves the fault lies anyplace but within ourselves. We say, "Oh, I really do want to obey God—but I have needs that must be met" or "I asked God to get me out of this situation, and He didn't, so I just had to lie; God left me no choice" or "God hasn't answered my prayers to provide what I need, so I'm going to have to rely on my own schemes and ingenuity." You may not verbalize it, but on some level, that is how we all think when we take refuge in Egypt instead of the Lord.

Abraham had built an altar in Bethel and there he called on the Lord—but then he moved away from Bethel. Not far, just a bit south, to the Negev, away from his neighbors, the Canaanites. But the Negev is on the way to Egypt. Abraham should not have left his altar in Bethel. He should have stayed in Canaan and trusted the Lord to deal with the Canaanites.

The Lord personally appeared to Abraham and made promises to him. Abraham had put his faith in God when God told him to leave his home in Ur of the Chaldeans and make a pilgrimage to a new land. But later he drifted. He rationalized. He moved south. And when the famine came, Abraham didn't look north toward his altar in Bethel. He looked south toward Egypt.

Soon he made the fateful decision to go down to Egypt for help in his time of need. Before he knew it, Abraham was leaving the land God had promised him and was seeking his help from the godless Egyptians instead of from God Himself.

Before he even set foot on Egyptian soil, Abraham began to scheme and devise a lie. He told his beautiful wife, "When the Egyptians see you . . . they will kill me but will let you live. Say you are my sister, so that I will be treated well for your sake and my life will be spared because of you." Then they went into Egypt.

> When Abram came to Egypt, the Egyptians saw that Sarai was a very beautiful woman. And when Pharaoh's officials saw her, they praised her to Pharaoh, and she was taken into his palace. He treated Abram well for her sake, and Abram acquired sheep and cattle, male and female donkeys, male and female servants, and camels.
>
> But the LORD inflicted serious diseases on Pharaoh and his household because of Abram's wife Sarai. So Pharaoh summoned Abram. "What have you done to me?" he said. "Why didn't you tell me she was your wife? Why did you say, 'She is my sister,' so that I took her to be my wife? Now then, here is your wife. Take her and go!" Then Pharaoh gave orders about Abram to his men, and they sent him on his way, with his wife and everything he had. (Gen. 12:14–20)

Abraham lied and he placed his wife's honor in jeopardy. When the passage says that the Egyptian officials "praised her to Pharaoh, and she was taken into his palace," it doesn't mean she got to take a tour of the place. It means she became one of the concubines in Pharaoh's harem. Through his lying and scheming, Abraham had put his wife in a terrible spot.

## Six Steps to Egypt

There are six steps we take that draw us away from Bethel, from trusting in the Lord—six steps that lead us down toward Egypt, toward trusting in our own resources. If you identify with any of these six steps, please understand that it is never too late. You can come back today, right now, to the very heart of worship and fellowship with God.

### Step #1: We Begin to Rely Only on Human Logic

Notice the word *only* in step #1. There's nothing wrong with human logic. God invented logic. He gave us minds with which to think and reason and understand. But when we begin to use *only* human logic, we're heading for trouble.

When Abraham realized he was living in the land of famine, he reasonably and logically understood that his Canaanite neighbors were in the same fix he was in. He knew they would not go out of their way to help a stranger. They had enough trouble finding food for themselves. Abraham had a good, logical grasp of his situation.

What did he do in response? Did he go to the God who had appeared to him at Bethel? Did he ask for help from the God who had made the sevenfold promises to him? Did he ask for help from the God who had called him out of Ur and into Canaan? No, he didn't seek God's resources. Using only human logic, he turned his eyes southward, toward Egypt.

Human logic is fine for certain simple kinds of problems, but human logic is no match for desperate situations like a famine. Human vision can see only so far. Human logic can't see the bigger picture. When a problem is so big that only God can solve it, applying merely human logic will only make matters worse. We need God's perspective. He is greater than all our circumstances, and He has limitless power to solve all of our crises.

Numbers 13 tells the story of the twelve spies Moses sent into Canaan, Israel's future home, to scout the land.

When the spies returned with their report, ten were against crossing into Canaan. They said, "We look like weak little grasshoppers compared to the powerful Canaanites." They doubted the promises of God. Only two of the spies, Joshua and Caleb, saw the land through eyes of faith. They were rational, logical men, and they acknowledged the dangers and obstacles that lay before them. But they believed that God was greater than the Canaanites and greater than any obstacles in the land of Canaan. They said, in effect, "These Canaanites are no match for our God. Let's go take the land."

When we look at our circumstances through the eyes of logic, we often see ourselves as grasshoppers. Because we fail to open our eyes of faith, we are spiritually blind. Like the ten spies who returned from Canaan, we are in the majority—but it is a fearful, doubting majority. The place of blessing and victory is with the faithful minority, Joshua and Caleb.

David Roper, the director of Idaho Mountain Ministries, tells of a friend who asked someone, "How are you doing?" The other person replied, "I'm doing all right, under the circumstances." Roper's friend asked, "What are you doing under there?"[1] This is why we often feel defeated and discouraged. We are under the circumstances instead of being lifted up by an exuberant, confident faith in God.

Using only human logic, we fail to see the whole picture—and we end up under our circumstances instead of triumphing over them. Open your eyes of faith. Look at your circumstances from God's perspective. Stay in Bethel, close to the altar, close to the Lord. And whatever you do, stay out of Egypt.

## Step #2: We Cease to Worship

Ceasing to worship doesn't only mean that we stop attending church, although that is usually part of it. I mean that our personal times of worship and prayer become shorter, more infrequent, and less meaningful and sincere. Eventually, those quiet times with the Lord cease altogether. We stop talking to God, singing praises to God, and even thinking about God. We are becoming worldly. We are out in the spiritual desert that is our Egypt.

The name *Bethel* means "the house of God." Abraham built an altar there, and that place became "the house of God" where he met God and God spoke to him. Nowhere in Scripture does it say that when Abraham went to Egypt, he built an altar to God there as he had built in Bethel. We have no record of him worshiping God in Egypt. All we know is that he came up with a cockamamie scheme to deceive the Egyptians and save his own hide. Because of that scheme, Abraham left Egypt in humiliation.

When Abraham used only human logic, when he failed to worship God, he lost sight of the big picture. He lost sight of God and His power. When we leave our altar of worship, when we move away from Bethel and go down to Egypt, we lose sight of the joy of being in God's presence. We know we ought to worship Him, but the whole idea of worship now seems boring, like a chore—nothing but drudgery. It happens slowly and gradually, but soon we find that our perspective has become 100 percent Egyptian. We hardly remember what it was like to worship God and enjoy His presence.

Charles Haddon Spurgeon, that great preacher of yesteryear, was the publisher of a monthly magazine, *The Sword and the Trowel*. In the March 1887 issue, Spurgeon published an article called "The Down Grade," written by his friend Robert Shindler. Both Spurgeon and Shindler were opposed to a trend they saw among some ministers and churches of (in Spurgeon's words) "denying the proper deity of the Son of God, [and] renouncing faith in his atoning death."[2] Those who rejected these essential doctrines of the Christian faith were on a downgrade or slippery slope.

To Spurgeon, biblical truth is like the very highest point on a mountain. Stand on that high point, and we are at the pinnacle of the mountain. Stand on God's truth and you are at the pinnacle of truth. If we take one step away from the highest point on the mountain, in any direction, we are no longer at the pinnacle—we are on the downgrade or slope. In the same way, if we take one step away from God's truth, in any direction, we are on a slippery slope that ultimately leads downward to error and destruction.

If you have stepped away from God's truth, if you have slid down the slippery slope toward error, you can climb back up to the pinnacle. Place your trust in God. Come back to the heart of worship, the center of truth.

Many Christians mistakenly think that attending church for an hour or two on Sunday will give them victory throughout the week. The world is too powerful and the devil is too conniving for you to spend just an hour a week with God. Spend time in private worship and fellowship with the Lord, reading His Word and praying and listening for the still, small voice of His Spirit. And spend time in fellowship with other believers in a small group Bible study or prayer meeting. There's no substitute for daily fellowship with the Lord and midweek spiritual pick-me-ups with other believers. If you persevere in regular and even continual worship, you'll never find yourself drawn into that proverbial Egypt and the spiritual regression and defeat it represents.

### Step #3: We Become Pridefully Self-Sufficient

We look at our accomplishments, our education, our bank account, our possessions—and though we would probably not say it out loud, we might think, *I'm doing very well for myself. I've managed to accomplish all these things. Oh, by the way, thank You, Lord, for making me so talented and brilliant.* We pay lip service to God, but only because we think we should. We really feel we did it all ourselves.

Abraham probably thought to himself, *These dumb Egyptians* [though I'm Egyptian-born, I don't take that personally]. *I have them fooled. Pharaoh took my wife into his harem, and because of her, they're treating me like a prince and giving me sheep and cattle and donkeys and camels and servants! Do I know how to scheme or what? Now, if I could just think up a scheme to get my poor wife out of that harem. . . .*

Abraham didn't trust God to provide for him during the famine in Canaan, and he didn't trust God to protect him from Pharaoh. He forgot the promise of God. While he was in Egypt, he forgot all about counting stars. He took matters into his own hands and concocted a deceptive scheme with Sarah. When he was building an altar at Bethel, Abraham was a paragon of faith and virtue—but once he got to Egypt, he turned into a con man! And the first person Abraham conned was himself. He convinced himself that he wasn't really lying because he was telling a half-truth—and we've all engaged in self-deceptive rationalizations, haven't we? I know I have.

We learn of Abraham's rationalization for lying about Sarah in Genesis 20:11–12, where Abraham says, "I said to myself, 'There is surely no fear of God in this place, and they will kill me because of my wife.' Besides, she really is my sister, the daughter of my father though not of my mother; and she became my wife." He's trying to convince himself that he's not *really* lying by calling Sarah his sister because Sarah really is his *half* sister.

Abraham knows better. He knows that the most important information Pharaoh should have is not Sarah's next-of-kin but Sarah's marital status. And by not telling the truth about Sarah's marital status, Abraham is perpetrating a lie of omission. And a lie is a lie is a lie, no matter how you tell it or how you try to rationalize it.

God does not wink at lies. He might not allow the consequences of our lies to fall on us immediately. We may not suffer the consequences of our lies for a week, a month, or a year. He may give us time to repent. But God does not wink at sin. He forgives sin, but he does not wink at it. He forgives our lies when we confess them and repent of them, but forgiveness does not expunge the natural consequences that our lies bring down on us.

Abraham probably felt very clever and self-sufficient as he pulled the wool over the Egyptians' eyes—but he was not living by faith, he was not trusting God, and he was not obeying God. He was deceiving, not believing.

### Step #4: Our Unconfessed Sin Leads to More Sin, Not Less

Abraham had ceased to be a pilgrim and had become a spiritual drifter. God had to intervene to protect the promise

He had made to Abraham, because Abraham was about to ruin God's plan. There is a world of difference between sinning and immediately repenting of that sin versus sinning and remaining in that sin. We tend to think of our sins as single isolated acts, but sin tends to accumulate other sins around it. Sin is like a snowball rolling down a snowy hill—it gets bigger and bigger and bigger.

We see this principle in the story of David and Bathsheba in 2 Samuel 11. First, David saw Bathsheba bathing on her rooftop, and he lusted. That was the initial sin. Then the sins began to snowball. He sent for her and committed adultery with her—another sin. Then he tried to cover up his sin with lies—more and more sins. He tried to manipulate and deceive Bathsheba's husband, Uriah the Hittite—still more sins. When his lies weren't working, he arranged to have Uriah murdered—the biggest sin of all. And this huge snowball of sin began with a single moment of lust, the equivalent of looking at internet porn.

Sin is dynamic, not static. It grows. And sin is always bigger and stronger than we are. There is only one force in the universe more powerful than sin, and that is the blood of Jesus Christ that He shed on Calvary. That's why only the blood of Jesus can cure our sin.

### Step #5: Our Sin Will Result in a Terrible Loss

Abraham thought he had devised a clever scheme, yet it ended in disaster. Abraham thought that Sarah was his meal ticket, and he could stretch out his negotiations with Pharaoh, getting richer and richer. But his plan backfired.

Now, I'm sure Abraham suffered a moment of absolute shock and horror when the Egyptian officials came for Sarah to take her to the Pharaoh's harem. His beloved wife might well have ended up having to defile herself with an act of adultery in order to save Abraham from death. Abraham didn't foresee where his plan would lead. Abraham's experience illustrates a biblical principle: whenever we choose our own way instead of obedience to God's way, we stand to lose everything that matters to us. I don't recall who said it, but this statement is devastatingly true: "We might be treated well when we seek friendship with the world, but that's a poor compensation for our losses."

For Abraham, there was no altar in Egypt, no fellowship with God in Egypt, and no new promise in Egypt. There was nothing for Abraham in Egypt but the betrayal of his marriage and the desolation of his household.

### Step #6: Our Unconfessed Sin Brings About a Rebuking Humiliation

The greatest blessing in the Christian faith is that God does not let go of His children. He never lets go of us. When He adopts us and gives us His name, we are cradled in the very palm of His hand. Nothing can take us out of those loving, fatherly hands. As children of God, we will not be lost even if we try, even if others try, even if the world tries and Satan tries. I'm so grateful to the Lord for this truth. I'm so grateful He pulled me out of my own proverbial Egypt and set me back beside the altar at Bethel.

But believe me, when God dragged me out of my Egypt, the heels of my shoes left deep ruts in the sand, because I did not want to leave my sin and selfish ambition and stubborn ways. God, by His grace, dragged me out of my Egypt and back to Himself, and that is the greatest gift He could give me.

Sometimes God drags us out of Egypt by revealing our sin and exposing our secrets. Think of your own worst sins, the secrets you hide from everyone. What if those sins were exposed? What if your spouse found out? What if your children knew? What if it became a news story and *everybody* found out? As horrifying as that may seem, it sometimes happens. It happens to presidents, members of Congress, judges, prominent pastors, celebrities, movie studio and TV moguls, and even ordinary folks.

If you want to sleep well every night, if you never want to worry about your secrets being exposed, come clean with God. Repent. Deal with your sin. Ask a trusted fellow believer to hold you accountable for the hidden corners of your life. Make sure that the person you are in public is the same person you are in private.

If sin brings about a deep humiliation in your life, you may think that's bad news. But it's really good news. God is allowing that rebuking humiliation in your life to bless you. It may feel as if God is destroying you, but in the eyes of eternity, He is saving your soul.

## Get Out of Egypt

In this account, we see the pagan Pharaoh being used by God to rebuke and humiliate Abraham in order to bring him back to his senses. This godless Egyptian king is straightening out Abraham, the friend of God. After the Lord inflicted disease on Pharaoh and his household, Pharaoh said to Abraham,

"What have you done to me? Why didn't you tell me she was your wife? Why did you say, 'She is my sister,' so that I took her to be my wife? Now then, here is your wife. Take her and go!"

It was a chastened and wiser Abraham who departed from Egypt and went back to Canaan where he belonged. Abraham returned to Bethel. Had he stayed in Canaan during the famine, he might have suffered, but his faith would have grown. He would have seen the supernatural, miraculous provision of God. Abraham stunted his own spiritual growth by going to Egypt.

When I was a young Christian and faced tough times and intimidating circumstances, I would cry to God in prayer: "Lord, get me out of this! Rescue me! Don't You care about me? Don't You love me? Have You abandoned me?"

But after decades of walking with the Lord, I know that seeming impossibilities are simply opportunities to grow deeper in my faith, opportunities to say, "I trust You, Lord, to lead me through this trial. I look forward to seeing Your mighty hand at work—even through this seemingly impossible situation."

Abraham discovered the hard way that it takes more grace to stay in Canaan than to run to Egypt. God loves us, and He wants to arrange our steps of faith to take us upward and onward with Him. Whether you are worshiping at Bethel or disobeying in Egypt or somewhere in between, whether you are at step #1 or step #6, you can still choose to go where God calls you and follow where He leads.

With all my heart, on the authority of God's Word, I beg you to act on this truth right now: it's never too late to return to the altar of worship.

# 4

# God's Promise Renewed

Janez Rus was a shoemaker in Yugoslavia when Nazi Germany invaded the country in 1941. His brother Joze joined the Yugoslavian resistance, but Janez chose to side with the Nazis. He cooperated with the Nazis and was vocal in his support of Adolf Hitler. His neighbors hated Hitler and despised Janez Rus for supporting the German invaders.

After Germany was defeated in 1945, Janez Rus disappeared. No one knew what happened to him. His brother had died in battle in 1943, and his mother and sister said they had no idea what happened to Janez. Years passed. People forgot all about Janez Rus.

One day in late 1977, the sister of Janez Rus visited a bakery in the village of Zalna and bought a large supply of bread. Someone who witnessed the purchase became suspicious and contacted the police. The police went to the farm where the sister lived and asked her why she had purchased so much bread. Only then did the sister break down and admit that her brother Janez was hiding in the attic of the farmhouse.

Janez came down and talked to the police. The police checked their records and found that no charges had ever been filed against the man. He was free to resume a normal life. He was sixty-four years old and had spent thirty-two years—half of his life—hiding in fear. Throughout all those years, he had never gone anywhere but the barn, the workshop, or the attic of that farm. He had never spoken to another human soul except his mother and sister. All that time, he feared that the Yugoslavian government would arrest him for his pro-Nazi activities.

Interviewed later by the Belgrade newspaper *Politka*, Janez Rus said that he would weep when he heard happy voices outside. When his mother died in 1966, he dared not attend her funeral for fear of being arrested. If the police had not come to investigate his sister's bread purchase, he said, he would have remained in hiding for the rest of his life. "Throughout these years I did nothing," he said, and then added, "Through the windows I looked down to the village in the valley. People seldom passed by our house. . . . There was no way out and I reconciled myself to the fate of a vanished man."

The newspaper interviewer observed that, because of his fear, Janez Rus had "sentenced himself to a punishment which no court could pass on him."[1] A baseless, needless fear was this man's prison for thirty-two years.

We all know what it feels like to be afraid. We have all experienced fear in one form or another. We each deal with fear in our own way, and we fear some things more than others. A fear that would terrorize one person might seem trivial and irrational to another. Some people experience a generalized sense of anxiety and fear and have trouble verbalizing why they feel that way.

Fear of failure keeps many people from reaching their full potential for God. Fear of criticism holds people back from accomplishing great things for God. Fear of the unknown chains some people down to what is comfortable and familiar—they are afraid to step out and live the adventure of faith.

But there's also a type of fear that seizes us only after we experience a major success or achieve a great goal. The Bible offers many examples of this kind of fear, and we are going to see this form of fear in the life of Abraham. We will see him show incredible bravery and courage in the face of mortal enemies. We will see him win a great victory. And then—we will see Abraham fall into a slump of fear and anxiety.

### The Rambo of Genesis

Abraham returned to the Negev from Egypt. He brought back with him the livestock, silver, and gold he had acquired in Egypt. He traveled about the land until he reached Bethel, where he had built the altar. There, once again, Abraham called upon the Lord in prayer. After getting spiritually off-track in Egypt, he was back in fellowship with God.

We see the godly and unselfish attitude of the spiritually renewed Abraham in an incident in Genesis 13, in which a dispute arose between Abraham's herdsmen and his nephew Lot's herdsmen. There was not enough water and grazing land for the herds and flocks of both men, so Abraham went to Lot and said, "Let's not have any quarreling between you and me, or between your herders and mine, for we are close relatives. Is not the whole land before you? Let's part company. If you go to the left, I'll go to the right; if you go to the right, I'll go to the left" (vv. 8–9).

Lot responded selfishly, choosing the lush and fertile land of the plain of the Jordan toward the cities of Sodom and Gomorrah. This left Abraham with the less productive and more arid land of Canaan.

In Genesis 14, we discover a side of Abraham we haven't seen before. It turns out that counting the stars of God's promises has turned Abraham into an Old Testament Rambo. There were terrorists in the land in those days, just as there are still terrorists in that land today. The terrorists invaded Sodom and Gomorrah and other towns in the Dead Sea area. They would ransack the whole town, kidnap people, and either hold them for ransom or enslave them. The terrorists from Elam, Goyim, Shinar, and Ellasar raided Sodom, where Abraham's nephew Lot lived, and they kidnapped Lot and his family. When word of Lot's abduction reached kind and generous Uncle Abraham, the old man knew it was time to swing into action. Though he was eighty-five years old, he was an octogenarian action hero.

There is nothing in the book of Genesis up to this point to suggest that Abraham had military training and experience. But Abraham was armed not only with the weaponry of that era but also with the promises of God. He knew that God had promised to make a great nation of him. Abraham was counting stars even when he could see none. He knew that, in order for God's promise to be kept, he would have to survive the battle—and this knowledge bolstered his confidence and courage.

Abraham assembled 318 warriors, men who had been born into his household and trained in the art of war. These were the kind of elite warriors we would now call Green Berets or Navy SEALs. He divided his forces and led them on a night raid to deliver Lot and the other hostages from the terrorists. Surrounding and storming the enemy camp in the dark of night, Abraham caught the terrorists off guard. Many of the enemy died in the fierce fighting. Others fled, taking the hostages with them.

With Abraham at the lead, his forces pursued the fleeing terrorists all the way to the town of Hobah, north of Damascus, a chase of more than a hundred miles. Abraham and his men caught up with the terrorists, fought and defeated them, and rescued Lot and the other hostages. They also recovered all the valuables the terrorists had looted from Sodom and the other towns.

When Abraham and his 318 elite warriors returned from the battle, you can be sure they received a hero's welcome, with a parade and a big party. The king of Sodom was there, and he was so grateful that he offered Abraham a blank check and invited him to fill in any amount. If Abraham had accepted the king's offer, he would have been a gazillionaire. He could have had the biggest ranch in the Middle East. Abraham probably found the king's offer tempting.

But Abraham remembered the promise God had made to him. He remembered that God had called him to count stars even when he could see none. He remembered that it was God who was going to bless him—not the king of Sodom. So Abraham turned the offer down flat, saying, "With raised hand I have sworn an oath to the LORD, God Most High, Creator of heaven and earth, that I will accept nothing belonging to you, not even a thread or the strap of a sandal, so that you will never be able to say, 'I made Abram rich'" (Gen. 14:22–23).

Though Abraham had failed God in Egypt, he had renewed his faith in God's promises at the altar at Bethel. Because he once again trusted in the promises of God, Abraham was no longer a con man, as he had been in Egypt. He was now a man of unswerving principle and rock-solid integrity. The same man who had accepted riches from Pharaoh under false pretenses now refused to accept even a thread or a sandal strap from the king of Sodom.

The reason many people are anxious and worried about financial security is that they leave God out of their finances. They have failed to recognize God as their one and only provider. When you come to the realization that no one but God can provide for you, then you cannot be insecure. Like Abraham, you can know your financial future is secure if you have placed all your trust in God.

## Jesus in Genesis

It's instructive to view this story from the point of view of Lot, Abraham's greedy nephew. Earlier, when given a choice by Uncle Abraham, Lot took the best land for himself. He left the less productive land to Uncle Abraham. Even though Lot had treated Abraham with selfish disregard, Abraham had selflessly taken up the sword, pursued and slaughtered the kidnappers, and rescued Lot and his family. I hope Lot was grateful to his uncle and ashamed of the way he had treated his generous uncle in the past.

Lot learned a great deal about Uncle Abraham's godly character during and after that rescue operation. His jaw must have dropped to the ground when he listened to the conversation between Abraham and the king of Sodom. The king tried to give Abraham a huge reward for defeating the terrorists—*and Abraham turned it down.*

I can imagine Lot thinking, *My uncle must be insane! Take the reward, Uncle Abraham! Or if you don't want it, pass it along to me!* But perhaps he didn't think such thoughts. Perhaps he had learned a lesson in character, integrity, and faith from his Uncle Abraham.

There's another fascinating scene that takes place in Genesis 14—the appearance of Melchizedek, King of Salem. The city-state of Salem is traditionally identified with Jerusalem, and the name *Salem* means "peace." Melchizedek appears seemingly out of nowhere, and he has brought out bread and wine. "He was priest of God Most High" (v. 18), Scripture tells us, and this priestly king proceeded to serve the bread and wine to Abraham. Then he blessed Abraham, saying:

> Blessed be Abram by God Most High,
>> Creator of heaven and earth.
> And praise be to God Most High,
>> who delivered your enemies into your hand.
>> (vv. 19–20)

You've undoubtedly noticed that the bread and wine are the elements of the Lord's Supper, which Jesus instituted just hours before going to the cross.[2] After Melchizedek blessed him, Abraham gave Melchizedek a tenth of everything he owned—not just 10 percent of his salary but of his entire net worth. Hebrews 7 tells us that Melchizedek is a symbolic type of Christ. The name *Melchizedek* means "king of righteousness," and the title *king of Salem* means "king of peace" (v. 2). I believe that Melchizedek was, in fact, a theophany—an Old Testament appearance of the Son of God in human form.

Why did Abraham give a tenth of everything to Melchizedek? I believe it's because Abraham recognized that Melchizedek was an appearance of God in human form. Isn't it interesting that Abraham tithed to God without being commanded to do so? Don't believe anyone who tells you that tithing is legalistic, that it's a practice that belongs to the law and is no longer needed in New Testament times. Abraham tithed to God four hundred years before the law was given to Moses. When Abraham tithed, there was no law— he gave of his own free will to God without being compelled by the law.

Psalm 110 has long been viewed by both Jews and Christians as a psalm of the Messiah. The psalmist writes that the Messiah shall be "a priest forever, in the order of Melchizedek" (v. 4). And that is what Jesus is to us. He is our king, our high priest, not of the order of Aaron, who sacrificed animals on an altar of stone, but of the order of Melchizedek. After sharing the bread and the wine with His disciples— representing His broken body and His shed blood—Jesus willingly laid down His life, not on an altar of stone but on a cross of wood.

Abraham has just experienced a spiritual and emotional high. He has achieved a great military victory. He has demonstrated his great faith in God's promise by refusing the plunder the king of Sodom offered him. He has met Melchizedek, the preincarnate Lord Jesus, and he has given a tenth of everything he owned to the king of Salem, the king of peace.

At this point in his life, Abraham's heart is so light and full of joy, he's practically walking two feet above the ground. But that ecstatic feeling won't last. He's about to tumble into an emotional and spiritual funk. He's about to sink into a pit of fear.

## Your Shield and Great Reward

Whenever God says to someone in the Bible, "Fear not," it's because that person is already afraid. God wants to replace that individual's fear with faith. We see this principle in the life of Joshua, who became the leader of Israel after the death of Moses. As Joshua is preparing to lead the Israelites across the Jordan River and begin the conquest of Canaan, God speaks to him and says, "Be strong and courageous. Do not be afraid; do not be discouraged, for the Lord your God will be with you wherever you go" (Josh. 1:9).

We see this principle in the life of Gideon as he was preparing to go into battle against the Midianites. The Bible tells us, "The Lord said to him, 'Peace! Do not be afraid'" (Judg. 6:23).

We also see this principle in the life of the prophet Elijah. When the captain of a band of Samarian soldiers came for Elijah to take him to the king, God tells him through an angel, "Go down with him; do not be afraid of him" (2 Kings 1:15).

Now, in Genesis 15:1, God comes to Abraham in a vision and says, "Do not be afraid, Abram. I am your shield, your very great reward."

Why, after experiencing such a great military and spiritual victory, is Abraham suddenly afraid? There is a paradoxical fear that people experience after a major success or achievement. It's an irrational kind of fear, striking when a person should feel confident, happy, on top of the world. That's the kind of fear Abraham experienced at the beginning of Genesis 15.

You may have undergone such an experience yourself. You may have gone through a difficult but rewarding time when God enabled you to overcome opposition or weariness or temptation or enormous odds. Now you are feeling the afterglow of accomplishing a major goal—and you are also feeling physically, emotionally, and spiritually spent. You are victorious—yet you are also vulnerable. And that is when you are attacked by a sudden emotional letdown, a physical exhaustion, a spiritual oppression.

Satan knows when we are vulnerable. He knows that his attacks hit hardest right after we experience victory and success. That is the moment we are filled with joy and pride, that is when our guard is down, and that is his moment of opportunity.

Nineteenth-century novelist Jean Paul observed, "A timid person is frightened before a danger, a coward during the time, and a courageous person afterward."[3] This could certainly be said of Abraham. He was not timid. He was not a coward. His fear didn't hit him until *after* he was victorious in battle. And God, seeing that Abraham is sinking into a pit of fear, comes to him and says, "Do not be afraid, Abram. I am your shield, your very great reward." This incident illustrates a principle I have often observed over more than fifty years of walking with the Lord: *God knows our needs before we do*, and He ministers accordingly. There are times when the Lord ministers to me, and I'm not even aware that I have a need. Suddenly, I am facing that need and God is already meeting it. Amazed, I say to Him, "What a precious gift of your grace, Lord! You knew my need before I knew, before I even thought to pray!"

As Abraham stepped down from the pinnacle of victory, he was about to plunge into the depths of depression. God knew what was coming—and with His loving hand He graciously caught Abraham in midfall. I love the words of the Lord to Abraham because it tells us the emotional state Abraham was sinking into: "Do not be afraid, Abram. I am your shield, your very great reward."

A shield covers you and protects you from the assault of the enemy's weapons. God was saying, "You are under My impenetrable cover, Abraham. Satan's flaming arrows can't reach you because you are under My strong care. You are in My protection program. In order for your enemies to get to you, they have to come through Me first."

As if that weren't enough, God also says He is Abraham's "very great reward." All that God is, all that God has, is our great reward.

"Under My protective cover," God was saying to Abraham—and to us—"you're not only in My protection program, but when you receive Me, I will satisfy your lonely heart, I will fill your empty void, I will give joy to the joyless, I will vindicate the righteous, I will supply all your needs according to the riches of Christ Jesus in glory." When we trust God as our true provider, when we trust Him with our future needs, our past sorrows, our guilt and shame, our tithes and offerings, He is going to give Himself to us—and He is everything we need.

When God is our great reward, it means we will share in everything God has. What does God have? Everything in the universe. Heaven and earth. The solar system. The galaxies. Everything.

Abraham had already received many revelations from God. Many more revelations lay ahead of him. Though Abraham knew God only by the name *El Shaddai*, he experienced the many-faceted character of the God who would later be known as *Jehovah-Jireh* ("the LORD who provides," who gives us everything we need), *Jehovah-Rapha* ("the LORD who heals," who even opens the womb of childless women), and *Jehovah-Nissi* ("the LORD our banner," who leads us to victory in battle). The Lord revealed Himself to Abraham in each of these facets, and Abraham's life changed with each new revelation.

Abraham even came to know God as his Abba, his loving Father. The apostle Paul writes about the profound nature of our relationship to our Heavenly Father: "Now if we are children, then we are heirs—heirs of God and co-heirs with Christ, if indeed we share in his sufferings in order that we may also share in his glory" (Rom. 8:17). That is one of the most amazing passages in all of Scripture. I can't read it without a tingling sense of excitement.

We are heirs of God. We inherit everything He is and everything He has. It's not like being an earthly heir in which we get a portion of the estate of someone who dies. There are billions of other believers, past and present and future and all around the world—but that doesn't mean our share of God's inheritance is measured in billionths of an estate. No, we inherit *everything* that belongs to God and *everything* God is! And so does every other believer.

You can live your life secure in Him, never having to worry about financial security, physical security, or the security of your salvation. No matter what happens in life, you are anchored in God. You don't have to live in fear, uncertainty, and anxiety anymore. You can rest in His presence.

## A Promise Renewed

After God promised that He would be Abraham's shield and great reward, Abraham yearned for reassurance.

> But Abram said, "Sovereign Lord, what can you give me since I remain childless and the one who will inherit my estate is Eliezer of Damascus?" And Abram said, "You have given me no children; so a servant in my household will be my heir."
> Then the word of the LORD came to him: "This man will not be your heir, but a son who is your own flesh and blood will be your heir." He took him outside and said, "Look up at the sky and count the stars—if indeed you can count them." Then he said to him, "So shall your offspring be."
> Abram believed the LORD, and he credited it to him as righteousness. (Gen. 15:2–6)

God had already promised to be Abraham's shield and great reward. But Abraham's response is not one of relief and confidence but of doubt and disappointment. You can probably empathize with Abraham. I know God understood Abraham's emotions. God made a promise fifteen years earlier when Abraham was seventy years old. Abraham wasn't getting any younger, and Sarah's biological clock was ticking as well—*ticktock, ticktock.* So it's not surprising that Abraham had moments of doubt.

Abraham was saying, in effect, "Lord, You are sovereign, and Your will is absolute. But You made a promise, and fifteen years have gone by and I'm running out of time. If I were to die right now, my servant would inherit all that I have. When is the promise going to be fulfilled?"

Who of us would have Abraham's patience with an unfulfilled promise? But throughout that time, Abraham continued to count stars when he could see none.

I can imagine that Abraham may have even told people, "God has promised to make a great nation of me." When people would ask, "Then where is your son? How are you going to become a great nation if you have no heir, no descendants? You are childless and your wife is past her childbearing years!" Abraham would say, "Just wait. You'll see." But after fifteen years, Abraham grew tired of the looks people gave him, the snickering behind his back, the friends who pitied him and questioned his sanity.

I think I can identify with Abraham. When I was eighteen, I knew that God had made a promise to me, a promise that he would supernaturally deliver me from a particularly difficult situation. I made the mistake of sharing this promise with some Christian friends—and I learned that I needed to be more careful what I shared with my friends, even if they were Christians. After I told them about God's promise to me, some of them went to my older brothers and told them what I had said. They told my brothers, "We're really concerned about Michael's state of mind. He thinks he's hearing God speaking to him, and we're afraid he's going to do something foolish."

I later heard what these friends had said to my brothers about me. I was very hurt by it, and I went to the Lord in prayer, pouring out my wounded feelings before Him.

It wasn't long afterward that God fulfilled His promise to me—exactly as He had said.

In sharing this, I want to make it clear that we must always be careful when we think we are hearing God speaking to us within our own spirit. It is easy to mistake our own desires for the voice of God. The voice of God within us will never promise anything or urge us to do anything that contradicts His Word. Always test any inner leading you receive against what is written in the Bible.

At the same time, we should not be too quick to dismiss another Christian's claim that God has spoken to him or her. We shouldn't be too quick to say, "I think he's got a mental problem" or "I think she's mistaking her emotions for God's voice." God still speaks to believers today, just as He spoke to believers in Bible times.

## Prepare to Be Amazed

In Genesis 15, Abraham was doing his estate planning, and he decided to share his plan with God. He said, "I remain childless and the one who will inherit my estate is Eliezer of Damascus. . . . You have given me no children; so a servant in my household will be my heir" (vv. 2–3). Abraham was still looking for an assurance from God that His promise had not been revoked.

God's response was kind and gracious, and He renewed the promise He had made to Abraham fifteen years earlier in Ur of the Chaldeans. There, God had promised to make a great nation of Abraham. In renewing this promise, God tells Abraham, "Look up at the sky and count the stars—if indeed you can count them. . . . So shall your offspring be."

Then, the Scriptures tell us Abraham believed the Lord, and the Lord credited Abraham's faith as righteousness. That is such an amazing, rich, and profound statement that I could write an entire book on that statement alone (and perhaps, one day, I shall).

Here's the truly astounding aspect of God's promise to Abraham: it was 100 percent God's doing, and zero percent Abraham's. God gave Abraham the faith to believe in the promise. Then God gave Abraham credit for believing! Isn't that just like our God? He does everything. All we have to do is receive His grace.

It doesn't matter who you are. It doesn't matter the degree of despair you feel. It doesn't matter how long you have been waiting. You can begin to trust Him afresh today—right now, this very moment.

Remember the story of Peter and his encounter with the risen Lord Jesus in John 21:1–6. Peter and a half dozen other disciples were out in their fishing boat on the Sea of Galilee. They had been fishing all night but had caught nothing.

Early the next morning, Jesus called to them from the shore, "Friends, haven't you any fish?"

"No," they answered.

Then Jesus said, "Throw your net on the right side of the boat and you will find some."

Peter and the other disciples knew that this was when the fish were sleeping. They had no hope of catching any fish—but on the strength of the Lord's word, they cast their nets. Then they tugged on them and found the nets so heavy with fish they could hardly haul them in.

Cast your net of prayer into the sea of God's promises—even if you have no hope, even if you see no glimmer of a chance that your prayer will be answered. If you are praying according to God's promises in His Word, He will deliver. He may delay, but He will not deny His promises.

Cast your net. Trust His promises. And prepare to be amazed.

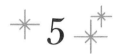

# The God Who Makes Covenants

Oliver Cromwell was one of the most powerful men ever to govern the Commonwealth of England, Scotland, and Wales. Born in 1599, he was a military and political leader during some of England's most turbulent years. He experienced a dramatic conversion in his late twenties and became an intensely devout Christian. In a letter to a cousin, Cromwell wrote, "Blessed be His Name for shining upon so dark a heart as mine! You know what my manner of life hath been. Oh, I have lived in and loved darkness and hated the light . . . yet God had mercy on me. O the riches of His mercy!"[1]

After his conversion, Cromwell devoted himself to the Puritan sect of Christianity. He believed God had called him to be a godly leader. He fought as a commander in the English Civil War. As a result of that war, the monarchy was abolished and a protectorate form of government (a benevolent dictatorship) was established with Cromwell as Lord Protector. His tenure was controversial; some saw him as a hero, others as a tyrant. Cromwell served as Lord Protector from 1653 until his death on September 3, 1658.

In the final hours of his life, Cromwell lay on his deathbed while a storm raged outside. Knowing the end was near, the fifty-nine-year-old Cromwell called his wife and grown children around him. What was on his mind in the final hours of his life? God's covenant with the human race.

"The Covenant of God," he told his children weakly. "It is holy and true—it is holy and true—it is holy and true! Who made it holy and true? The Mediator of the Covenant! [That is, Jesus.] The Covenant is one. And even if I do not, He remains faithful. Love not the world. No, my children, live like Christians. I leave you the Covenant to feed upon."[2]

These are worthy thoughts for a devout Christian on his deathbed.

The Bible speaks of God as a covenant-making God. He makes covenants with people, and He has made a series of covenants with the human race in the Old and New Testaments. The covenant that Oliver Cromwell spoke of on his deathbed is the new covenant that Jesus instituted at the Last Supper when He said, "This cup is the new covenant in my blood, which is poured out for you" (Luke 22:20). As Hebrews 9 tells us, "For this reason Christ is the mediator of a new covenant, that those who are called may receive the promised eternal inheritance—now that he has died as a ransom to set them free from the sins committed under the first covenant" (v. 15).

The greatest of God's covenants with the human race is the cross of Jesus Christ. Through the blood of Jesus, shed upon the cross, God the Father invited everyone who would believe in Him to receive the gift of eternal life. He took the punishment for our sins upon Himself. The new covenant is the good news of the Christian gospel.

What is the gospel? Is it the message that God so loved the world that anyone who sincerely believes in one of many religions of the world is going to be saved? No, that is not the gospel. Is it the message that God so loved the world that everyone in the world unconditionally gets to go to heaven? No, that is not the gospel either. Is it the message that God so loved the world that anyone who tries to live a good life will be saved? No, none of these notions, which are very popular in our culture today, is the gospel.

The gospel of the new covenant has a very specific meaning, which Jesus Himself defined when He told a man named Nicodemus, "For God so loved the world that he gave his one and only Son, that *whoever believes in him* shall not perish but have eternal life" (John 3:16, emphasis added). That's the true gospel. It means that anyone who believes in Jesus as Lord will be saved, and anyone who rejects Jesus will be condemned. It's very important—eternally important—that we understand what God's covenants mean and what they do not mean.

## Covenants between Unequals

In all of life, there are many kinds of agreements and covenants we make with one another. Most are agreements between two equals. In marriage, a husband and wife, two equals, make a covenant of marriage before God. He is the primary witness to the covenant, and the congregation is the secondary witness. Thanks to the armies of lawyers who now run our society, even the purchase of a ninety-nine-cent app for your smartphone involves a hundred-page "end user license agreement" you must agree to before purchasing the app (but who reads it?).

Throughout the Bible, God makes a series of covenants. But the covenants between God and human beings are unlike the covenants we make with other people. A covenant between God and humanity cannot be a covenant between two equals. It is, by definition, a covenant between two very unequal parties. In His covenants with human beings, God does all the heavy lifting. He takes upon Himself 100 percent of the responsibility for fulfilling the covenant.

God made a covenant with Adam and Eve in Genesis 3:15, in which He promised that Jesus the Messiah would come and He would crush the head of the serpent, the devil. In Genesis 9:13–15, God made a covenant with Noah after the flood and promised never to destroy all life in the world with floodwaters again. In Genesis 12:1–7, God made a sevenfold covenant with Abraham, calling him to leave Ur of the Chaldeans and move to Canaan and promising to make a great nation of him.

Now, in Genesis 15, God makes another covenant with Abraham. Following Abraham's battle with the terrorist kings, his rescue of his nephew Lot, and his amazing meeting with Melchizedek, King of Salem, Abraham goes into a spiritual slump. He looks to God for reassurance that He is still going to keep the covenants He has made with Abraham. God not only assures Abraham but also tells him, "Do not be afraid, Abram. I am your shield, your very great reward" (v. 1). God wants Abraham to know that, no matter what happens, no matter how long it might take, God will keep His word to Abraham.

When Abraham needs further reassurance, God shows Abraham the stars in the night sky and says, "So shall your offspring be." Abraham believed, and God credited Abraham's faith to him as righteousness. Then God went on to confirm His identity to Abraham:

> He also said to him, "I am the LORD, who brought you out of Ur of the Chaldeans to give you this land to take possession of it."
>
> But Abram said, "Sovereign LORD, how can I know that I will gain possession of it?" (vv. 7–8)

There's a principle in this passage we can learn from Abraham: God is not offended by our candid, honest prayers. God was not offended by Abraham's unloading of his burdens before the Lord. He was not offended when Abraham honestly confessed his worries and doubts. He was not offended by Abraham's innermost thoughts and emotions. God already knows when we have emotional volcanoes exploding inside us—we certainly won't offend Him by admitting what He already knows. He wants us to verbalize it. Our honesty with God is the mark of a healthy and trusting relationship with Him.

### Belief, Unbelief, and a Covenant Written in Blood

We respect God for who He is—almighty God, maker of heaven and earth. He is worthy of glory and praise. Yet this same almighty God is also our Abba, our Father. He does not expect His children to address Him in formal terms, in stuffy King James English, making a pretense of a perfect faith that we don't really feel. We can pour out our hearts to Him, as a child speaks to an earthly mother and father.

Abraham addresses God with respect: "Sovereign LORD, how can I know that I will gain possession of it?" But he doesn't hesitate to tell God plainly and candidly that he is troubled with doubts. "How can I know?" he asks. This is not an expression of unbelief—God has already credited Abraham's faith to him as righteousness. This is an admission that while Abraham believes God's promises, his willingness to believe is also being assailed and undermined by his human frailty.

Abraham is like the anguished father in Mark 9 who begged Jesus to heal his demon-possessed son. Jesus told the man, "Everything is possible for one who believes." And the man responded, "I do believe; help me overcome my unbelief!" (vv. 23–24). And Jesus acted on the man's faith and healed his son.

In contrast to this account is the story of Zechariah in Luke 1. Zechariah and his wife, Elizabeth, were in a situation very similar to that of Abraham and Sarah—a childless couple, both very advanced in years and beyond childbearing age. When an angel told Zechariah that God was going to give them a son, who would be John the Baptist, Zechariah simply didn't believe it. Instead of expressing faith hemmed in by questions and doubts, as Abraham did, Zechariah expressed sheer skepticism.

So God struck Zechariah speechless because of his unbelief. Not all questioning is unbelief. Abraham asked questions out of a place of faith. Zechariah's questions came from a place of skepticism, but his faith grew enormously after his son John was born.

When Jesus hung dying on the cross, He experienced His own moment of questioning. He was the Son of God, the Second Person of the Trinity, who had been one with the Father throughout eternity. Yet He asked the most profound why question ever asked: "My God, my God, why have you forsaken me?" (Matt. 27:46). He knew the answer, yet He asked why. To ask why is not to express unbelief. God understands our weaknesses, our questions, our doubts—and He accepts them.

That is why, in response to Abraham's question, God enacted a covenant with him. God knew that Abraham was weak, like you and me, so He graciously gave Abraham a visible sign of the covenant. God often makes His promises visible to us in a memorable way. When He made the covenant with Noah after the flood, He gave Noah the sign of a rainbow. When Gideon came to God in prayer, seeking a sign of His promise of victory over the Midianites, God twice gave him a sign through the fleece Gideon had spread out on the ground. God responded to Hezekiah's request in 2 Kings 20 by making the shadow of a sundial move backward. And when Jesus told His disciples about a new covenant God was making—a covenant written in His blood—Jesus gave them the elements of Holy Communion: the bread representing His body, the wine representing His blood.

Here, in Genesis 15, God again makes His covenant visible and memorable in a dramatic way.

## The Symbols of a Covenant

There have been times in my life when I felt God calling me to take a certain step of faith—but I wasn't absolutely sure

91

if it was God calling me or if it was my own will. I have learned that before I run headlong into some venture, I need to stop and pray, "Lord, please show me a sign. Let me know for certain that this venture is of You." And God graciously gives me a clear sign.

A *covenant*, simply defined, is a promise. In Genesis 15, the covenant is a promise made by God to Abraham. I prefer the word *promise* rather than *covenant* because a covenant sometimes conveys the idea of a deal or bargain made between two people: "If you do this for me, I'll do that for you." When God makes a covenant with us, there is no deal, no bargain. We human beings have nothing to offer Him in return, and we have a miserable track record of keeping our end of any bargain.

God's promise to Abraham was unilateral (He took it all upon Himself), eternal (not temporary or just for a season), and based on His grace (not on our performance). What a great God we worship! Abraham did not deserve the promise of God—and we do not deserve the promise of salvation by grace through faith in Jesus Christ. All the sevenfold promises that God made to Abraham, and all the promises that God has made to us, are fulfilled in Jesus Christ. Today, the descendants of Abraham are vastly more numerous than the stars Abraham could see in the night sky, because the descendants of Abraham are all those who have trusted in Jesus for their salvation. That is the unilateral, eternal, gracious promise God made to Abraham.

In our Western culture, we are familiar with covenants that have been established in writing. Through the ages and across the world, however, there are many different ways that cultures make binding promises. In many cultures, from Africa and the Middle East to the Pacific Islands and ancient North America, blood covenants have been common. The notion of a blood covenant is that the participants cut their flesh and mingle their blood (which we now know is an effective way to spread infection and disease). Blood gives us life, so the mingling of blood represents the sharing of life. The participants to the covenant become "blood brothers," bonded to one another by shared blood.

In other cultures, a covenant might be formally initiated with a binding oath—a vow with dire consequences attached if the oath taker violates his vow. In some cultures, the two partners to the covenant might share a ceremonial meal. The shared food symbolizes a bond of shared life.

Conveying the biblical idea of a covenant to other cultures has sometimes been a challenge for Bible translators. For example, the Shilluk people in the Nile River region of southern Sudan have no words for covenant or forgiveness in their language. Bible translators had no Shilluk words to express the idea of a covenant of forgiveness between God and humanity.

Translator and linguist Eugene Nida interviewed many Shilluk people to find out how to best express this idea. He learned that the Shilluk people had a tribal custom for settling disputes between a plaintiff and a defendant. The dispute would be heard before a tribal court, the matter would be decided, then the plaintiff would signify that he accepted the ruling and forgave the defendant by spitting on the ground at the feet of the defendant. This meant the matter was closed and the grievance was settled forever. This was a binding covenant of forgiveness.

When the Bible translators learned of this custom, they were able to describe God as the One who spits on the ground at your feet—the One who settles the sin problem, forgiving and forgetting our sins forever. This was a concept the Shilluk people could understand.[3]

The symbols of a covenant may differ from culture to culture, but the meaning is always the same. A covenant is a promise that binds the partners together in two ways: it creates a bond of relationship, and it creates a bond of obligation. In the case of God's covenants with humanity (including His covenants with Abraham), the obligation was unilateral: God obligated Himself to keep His promises. But the relationship aspect of God's covenant is mutual: God enters into a relationship with us, and we enter into a relationship with God.

## An Indelible Covenant

In the Middle Eastern culture of Abraham's day, a covenant was based on a ceremony. In those times, people would kill an animal and cut it in half as part of the covenant ceremony. They would then place the two halves across from each other with a path in between. The two parties to the agreement would walk the path between the two halves of the animal carcass. The contract was conducted in that space. In Genesis 15, God comes down to Abraham's level and makes a covenant with him in terms a man of the ancient Middle East could understand.

Abraham didn't have to do anything. God Himself would enter that space alone and make His covenant promise to Abraham in a tangible and symbolic way.

94

So the LORD said to him, "Bring me a heifer, a goat and a ram, each three years old, along with a dove and a young pigeon."

Abram brought all these to him, cut them in two and arranged the halves opposite each other; the birds, however, he did not cut in half. Then birds of prey came down on the carcasses, but Abram drove them away.

As the sun was setting, Abram fell into a deep sleep, and a thick and dreadful darkness came over him. Then the LORD said to him, "Know for certain that for four hundred years your descendants will be strangers in a country not their own and that they will be enslaved and mistreated there. But I will punish the nation they serve as slaves, and afterward they will come out with great possessions. You, however, will go to your ancestors in peace and be buried at a good old age. In the fourth generation your descendants will come back here, for the sin of the Amorites has not yet reached its full measure."

When the sun had set and darkness had fallen, a smoking firepot with a blazing torch appeared and passed between the pieces. On that day the LORD made a covenant with Abram and said, "To your descendants I give this land, from the Wadi of Egypt to the great river, the Euphrates—the land of the Kenites, Kenizzites, Kadmonites, Hittites, Perizzites, Rephaites, Amorites, Canaanites, Girgashites and Jebusites." (Gen. 15:9–21)

God gave instructions, and Abraham faithfully carried them out. He brought the animals, cut them in two, arranged them, then kept the wild scavenger animals from stealing the sacrifices.

Next, God placed Abraham in a deep sleep, and a "dreadful darkness" descended on him. As Abraham slept, God spoke to him, and He alone walked in the space between the animal parts. In this way, God signified that He took full responsibility for keeping the promises He had made.

What is the significance of the slain and divided animals? According to that culture, this ceremony announced to the world that if any party to the covenant broke his vow and violated the covenant, what happened to the animal would be done to the covenant breaker. The shedding of blood was a clear indication of the seriousness with which the covenant was viewed.

When God passed through the midst of the animals that had been cut in half, He passed through the shed blood that had pooled on the ground. In passing through that blood, He foreshadowed the blood of Jesus Christ shed upon the cross—the blood which alone can save us from our sins. When Jesus hung upon the cross, His life's blood spilling down upon the ground of Calvary, He made it possible for everyone who would believe on Him to be saved—and God the Father confirmed His covenant with Abraham.

With the ceremony and symbols of the slain and divided animals, God assured Abraham that He was not only a covenant-*making* God but also a covenant-*keeping* God. The New Testament book of Hebrews tells us:

> When God made his promise to Abraham, since there was no one greater for him to swear by, he swore by himself, saying, "I will surely bless you and give you many descendants." And so after waiting patiently, Abraham received what was promised. (Heb. 6:13–15)

In this ceremony, God shows Abraham a smoking firepot (also called a refiner's fire), and then He shows him a blazing torch. These fiery images symbolize God's perseverance. His promises are unilateral, eternal, and gracious. When God promises to write our names in His Book of Life at the moment we receive Jesus as Lord and Savior, He doesn't write our names with a pencil and erase them when we sin. He writes our names in the Book of Life with something more permanent and indelible than India ink: the precious and powerful blood of Jesus.

God's promise is eternal. His love is eternal. He loved us long before we ever responded to His love. Unlike so many forms of human love, God's love does not change with whims and moods. His love is not limited to a moment of time or space. His love is always "for better or for worse," His better and our worse. His promise of love and forgiveness will never fail us.

Even if we disobey Him, He loves us. That doesn't mean our disobedience will not leave scars. If a mother tells her little boy, "Don't touch the stove or you will be burned," and the boy disobeys, his mommy will forgive him. But the scars of his disobedience will remain, possibly for life, as a continual reminder. So it is when we disobey God.

## What Cost Us Nothing Cost Him Everything

One truth we should take away from the ceremony in Genesis 15 is that the God of the Old Testament is identical to the God of the New Testament. He is one God, and He doesn't change. Don't let anyone mislead you with the notion that the God of the Old Testament is the God of wrath but the God of the New Testament is the God of love. That is a lie from the lips of Satan himself. God is the same yesterday, today, and tomorrow. The grace that God showed Abraham through this ceremony of the covenant is the very same grace God has shown to you and me through His Son, Jesus, in the New Testament.

God demonstrates His love for us by choosing us, electing us, and bringing us to Himself. He demonstrates His love for us as He perseveres with us through our times of foolishness and disobedience. He loves us with a steadfast love, not an emotional or changeable love.

Most of us have a very distorted view of the love of God. I hear people describe God's love as changeable and unpredictable—"I think God is mad at me because of my sin" or "I think I missed out on God's will for my life, so He has turned His back on me." That's not a description of the God of the Bible. That is simply imputing changeable human emotions to our loving, unchanging God.

Why do we have such a distorted view of God? I believe that, in part, it's because we have a distorted view of love. People say, "I've fallen in love!" or "I've fallen out of love." They seem to think that love is something we jump into or out of, like getting in and out of the shower. That's not how God loves us. His love is unilateral, eternal, and full of grace. He carried our sorrows, forgave our sins, removed our guilt, and took our punishment upon Himself. Does that sound like a God who falls in and out of love with us on a whim?

God's love is not seasonal or changeable. It's for all eternity. His love will take us all the way to heaven with Him. That's why Paul could say, "Who shall separate us from the love of Christ?" Answer: No one! "Shall trouble or hardship or persecution or famine or nakedness or danger or sword?" Answer: Nothing![4]

God didn't forgive you and me yesterday so that He could turn against us today. We can take comfort in knowing that His love is completely undeserved. I don't deserve His love, you don't deserve His love, and believe it or not, that's *good news*. Nothing we do is going to make us any less deserving than we already are. Now, if we sin, there will be consequences to pay, there will be damage inflicted on the closeness of our relationship with God. But God won't love us any more or any less.

When God called Abraham and promised to make a great nation of him, Abraham was an idol worshiper in Ur of the Chaldeans. What had this pagan idol worshiper ever done to deserve God's favor and God's promise? Nothing. God called Abraham according to His own sovereign election and grace.

When God called you and me to leave our sinfulness and rebellion and to follow Him, what had we ever done to deserve His grace? Nothing. I will confess to you, in my early life, I rebelled against God. I shook my fist at Him, and I ran away from Him just as Jonah did. If I deserved anything, it was judgment. Yet I have received grace upon grace upon grace from the hand of God, and so have you. God called you and me according to His own sovereign election and grace.

Many Christians today misunderstand the doctrine of the grace of God, and they have turned it into a license to sin. What does the grace of God mean? It means simply that it pleased God to save you, and it pleased God to save me. God didn't choose us because we have so much to offer Him or because He really needs wonderful people like us on His team. He chose us because He is sovereign, and He has every right in the universe to choose us—or not—simply because He is God and this is His universe.

It cost Him everything to save us. It cost us nothing. Jesus didn't walk through this world without sacrificing. It cost Him everything. He didn't *make* a sacrifice for our sin, He *was* the sacrifice for our sin. His body was tortured, torn, and broken, and He bled to death for our sin. He was so covered with the stain, filth, and stench of our sin that the Father had to turn away and leave the Son alone to suffer and die.

Jesus offered His own sinless body for sinners like us. His grace compelled me to come to Him. His love wooed me. That is why I promised God that I would spend my life thanking Him and praising Him and honoring Him and serving Him and lifting up His great name.

There is no name like the magnificent name of Jesus, the mediator of the new covenant in His blood. He loved us first, and He loves us to the end. His love is unilateral. His love is eternal. His love is gracious.

Thank God for the promise He made to Abraham—and to you and me. His promises never change.

# *6*

# The Chapter of Failure

The tragedy took place on New York's Long Island, but it could have happened anywhere in America. A van loaded with ten teenagers pulled up to the tracks as the crossing gate arms came down. Flashing red lights warned that a Long Island Railroad train was approaching. The five-car passenger train was traveling at sixty-five miles an hour. If the driver had waited less than a minute, the train would have passed, and he and his passengers would have been safely on their way.

It was about two in the morning, and the teens were returning home from a party. All ten had been classmates and friends since childhood, having attended local parochial schools together. Because it was dark, it was hard to judge the train's speed and distance. The driver probably wondered, *What if it's a long freight train? We could be stuck here for ten minutes.*

The impatient young driver made a fateful decision. He gunned the engine and swung the van around the gate and onto the tracks. There was no time for the engineer to slow the train, much less stop it.

The train hit the van like a battering ram, crumpling the metal shell, cutting the vehicle in two. The front section of the van tumbled 150 yards along the tracks. The rear axle and back end of the van hurtled off to the side of the tracks. When the van came to rest, nine teenage occupants, ages seventeen to nineteen, were dead. One seventeen-year-old girl survived with critical injuries.

A police officer investigating the tragedy said there was no indication that drugs or alcohol were involved. None of the kids had ever been in trouble with the law—not even a minor traffic stop. "They were nice young kids," he concluded sadly.[1]

Nine teens were dead and one badly injured. It was a senseless, needless tragedy.

The cause of the tragedy? Impatience.

## The Devastating Cost of Impatience

In Genesis 15, God dramatically reconfirmed His covenant with Abraham by walking through the middle of the sacrificed and divided animals whose blood foreshadowed the blood of Jesus Christ. You would think that after God had reaffirmed the promise in such a dramatic way, Abraham would be able to wait patiently, counting stars and trusting God to fulfill His covenant. Instead, in a moment of impatience, Abraham did an about-face—and stumbled headlong into the biggest mess he had ever made.

Here we are in the twenty-first century, four thousand years after Abraham's big mistake, and we are still experiencing tragedy after tragedy because of Abraham's impatience. If Abraham had not sinned through impatience with God's promise, many tragedies that are a part of our history would never have happened. The Muslim religion traces its cultural and religious lineage back to Abraham and his liaison with Sarah's handmaid Hagar (and Ishmael, who was born from that liaison). Events ranging from the wars of Islamic conquest of the seventh and eighth centuries to the terror attacks of September 11, 2001, would never have occurred if Abraham had not been impatient with God.

One of the lessons of Abraham's error is that we should never think our sin doesn't affect others. Our sin can impact not only the people around us but also generations yet unborn. Another lesson we should learn is that a time of testing often nips at the heels of a blessing. If you are being blessed right now—heads up! A test is just around the corner. This is a biblical principle, and I have seen this principle borne out in my own life many times.

If Genesis 15 can be called "The Chapter of Faith," Genesis 16 can be called "The Chapter of Failure." In chapter 15, Abraham walked by faith. In chapter 16, he walked by the flesh. In Genesis 15, he listened to God. In chapter 16, he listened to his wife.

Please understand, I am not being harder on Sarah than I am on Abraham. The ground is level between Abraham and Sarah. In Genesis 12, Abraham asked Sarah to lie for him as they were about to enter Egypt. That was his sin and the evidence of his lack of faith. Now in Genesis 16, Sarah comes to him and urges him to let go of his trust in God's promise.

This does not relieve Abraham of moral responsibility. He is responsible to do the right thing and to continue counting stars and trusting God, even if his wife urges him to sin. Let's look at the opening verses of Genesis 16:

> Now Sarai, Abram's wife, had borne him no children. But she had an Egyptian slave named Hagar; so she said to Abram, "The LORD has kept me from having children. Go, sleep with my slave; perhaps I can build a family through her."
> Abram agreed to what Sarai said. So after Abram had been living in Canaan ten years, Sarai his wife took her Egyptian slave Hagar and gave her to her husband to be his wife. He slept with Hagar, and she conceived.
> When she knew she was pregnant, she began to despise her mistress. (vv. 1–4)

You might find this surprising, but I believe that when Sarah urged Abraham to have intercourse with her maid Hagar, Sarah was truly engaging in a selfless and loving act toward her husband. I'll show you what I mean. To do that, I need to transport you four thousand years back in time. We have to go back in history, not merely to an earlier time but a vastly different culture, so that we can understand what took place between Abraham, Sarah, and Sarah's maid Hagar.

In order to rightly divide the Word of truth, we have to place this Scripture passage in its proper context. By *context*, I don't merely mean the verses that come before and the verses that come after. I mean we have to understand whom this text was written to and whom it was written about. We have to understand the times and the culture in which it was written. What did this passage intend to say? What were the cultural customs of that time? We can't understand what the Bible is saying today unless we understand what it was saying to the people it was written to.

In those days, in that culture, a man's standing in society was dependent on how many children he had. Abraham's status in his society and even his manhood were at stake. Sarah felt that Abraham was disgraced and humiliated in Middle Eastern society at that time because he had no son.

Sarah wanted the world to know that the reason they were not able to have children was that she was unable to conceive. It was her fault, not her husband's fault. Sarah sincerely believed that if she followed the cultural norms, she could give Abraham the son he wanted by means of her Egyptian servant girl Hagar.

The custom of having children through your slave or servant was fairly common in the ancient world. If the wife couldn't give her husband children, she would have her servant girl conceive, then the servant girl would deliver the baby on her mistress's lap. Through this polite fiction, women who were unable to conceive could have a child. This was legal and accepted by Middle Eastern society of that time, but it was not right in God's eyes.

In every culture, there are practices that are legal, but they are still wrong in God's eyes. Abortion is legal and accepted by society, but God says it is sin. Same-sex marriage is now legal in America, but God says it is contrary to His created order. Adultery and fornication and pornography, telling lies for career advantage, character assassination for political advantage, and many other vile acts are approved of and applauded in many corners of our society—but these acts are gravely sinful in the eyes of God.

Sarah urged her husband to commit an act of adultery in order to hurry God's promise along. I believe her motives were selfless—not sinless but at least selfless. Even though she sought to take the blame and stigma of childlessness off Abraham, she was urging and encouraging her husband to sin.

I believe that if anyone else had suggested that course of action to Abraham, he probably would have rejected it. But this suggestion came from Sarah herself. If she was advocating that he have relations with her maid in order to have a child, then (he probably reasoned) why should he argue with her? But in his heart, I believe Abraham knew it was wrong. He knew that having a son by another woman instead of his wife would not fulfill God's promise.

Abraham listened to Sarah's urging. He had relations with Hagar, and she conceived a son. He acted in impatience, apart from faith. And the result was disastrous.

## Good Intentions Are No Substitute for Obedience

Paul argues in Galatians 4 that it is critically important that we are spiritual descendants of Abraham through Sarah and Isaac—not through Hagar and Ishmael:

Tell me, you who want to be under the law, are you not aware of what the law says? For it is written that Abraham had two sons, one by the slave woman and the other by the free woman. His son by the slave woman was born according to the flesh, but his son by the free woman was born as the result of a divine promise.

These things are being taken figuratively: The women represent two covenants. One covenant is from Mount Sinai and bears children who are to be slaves: This is Hagar. Now Hagar stands for Mount Sinai in Arabia and corresponds to the present city of Jerusalem, because she is in slavery with her children. . . .

Now you, brothers and sisters, like Isaac, are children of promise. At that time the son born according to the flesh persecuted the son born by the power of the Spirit. It is the same now. But what does Scripture say? "Get rid of the slave woman and her son, for the slave woman's son will never share in the inheritance with the free woman's son." Therefore, brothers and sisters, we are not children of the slave woman, but of the free woman. (vv. 21–25, 28–31)

There is a powerful spiritual principle at work in the story of Abraham, Sarah, and Hagar—and profound spiritual symbolism. The spiritual descendants of Abraham, Ishmael, and the slave woman Hagar are slaves to the law of Moses given at Mount Sinai. But we, as spiritual descendants of Abraham, Isaac, and the free woman Sarah, are free indeed through faith in Jesus Christ.

In Genesis 15, Abraham told God that because he had no son, "the one who will inherit my estate is Eliezer of Damascus. . . . A servant in my household will be my heir." The Lord replied, "This man will not be your heir, but a son who is your own flesh and blood will be your heir." Then the Lord took Abraham outside and showed him the night sky. "Look up at the sky and count the stars," the Lord told Abraham. "So shall your offspring be."

Some people have tried to defend Abraham's liaison with Hagar by pointing out that God never told Abraham he would have a son by his wife Sarah. God only said that Abraham would have "a son who is your own flesh and blood."

God never told Abraham not to have a son with his wife's servant girl.

But God didn't have to be that specific. Abraham had only one wife, and his wife was Sarah. The fact that Abraham's son would be conceived by Sarah, his wife, was clearly implied by God and clearly understood by Abraham. There is no question that Abraham knew he was doing an end run on God's will by agreeing to Sarah's well-intentioned but sinful scheme. Good intentions are no substitute for obedience. Abraham knew that God intended for him to have a child by Sarah, but by this time, the waiting had become almost unbearable for them.

I would be the last person on earth to say that waiting is easy. I can sympathize with their anguish and even their growing impatience. Sarah looked at their situation and concluded, in effect, "Look at us! We're old! We're about ready for the nursing home, not a nursery! Everyone else our age is called Grandma and Grandpa, even Great-Grandma and Great-Grandpa—and we're supposed to wait for God to bring us a baby?"

The disappointment and impatience of Sarah and Abraham are understandable. But they crossed a line into disobedience when they decided to help God out by rushing His timetable. When we stop trusting God's promises, no matter how rational and well intentioned our reasons may sound, we are blaming God for our difficulties.

Have I ever been impatient with God's timing? Have I ever tried to speed up God's timetable? I have to confess—been there, done that. I freely confess that I can sometimes be as impatient as Abraham and Sarah. One of my greatest fears is that I will lose patience with God and try to hurry His will along. May it never be!

### God Doesn't Need Our Help

Read Genesis 16:2 carefully, and you'll see that Sarah is quite explicit in blaming God for their childlessness: "The LORD has kept me from having children," she says. And let's be honest; she's right. It was God who decided whether Sarah's womb would be fertile and open—or sealed shut. But instead of accepting God's will and waiting to see how He would fulfill His promise, she impatiently blamed God. In that moment, Sarah told Abraham, "Go, sleep with my slave; perhaps I can build a family through her."

Sometimes we do the worst things with the best of intentions. We tell ourselves, "At least my motive was good." But sin is sin is sin.

Question: Who is at fault here? Sarah or Abraham? Answer: Both! The only person not at fault was Hagar. She was a bond servant, a humble slave. She had to do as she was told. She had no authority whatsoever.

Now let me offer some counsel that I often give myself. When I am waiting for God to do the supernatural, I am careful not to attempt to do the natural. Don't try to help God. He doesn't need our help. Keep serving Him, living for Him, and waiting for Him.

By trying to help God and hurry His will along, Abraham and Sarah made a mess of things. Yes, God specializes in picking up the threads of our failures and weaving them into a beautiful tapestry of His grace. He is renowned for pasting together the pieces of our fractured lives into a beautiful mosaic of His love. That's the God whose handiwork we see in this passage. But our lives will be so much more pleasant, so much more effective, if we wait for God in obedience.

When my wife and I were younger and our children were little, my wife used to read nursery rhymes to them. I watched and listened, and I saw the wonder in the eyes of my children as she read to them. One of my children's favorite stories was about an egg-shaped fellow: "Humpty Dumpty sat on a wall, Humpty Dumpty had a great fall. All the king's horses and all the king's men couldn't put Humpty together again."

I remember one time listening to that rhyme and thinking, *Humpty Dumpty didn't need the king's horses or the king's men; Humpty Dumpty needed the king!*

You and I need the king, because the king can do what the king's horses and the king's men cannot do. Trust in God our king. Believe in Him. Be patient and wait for Him. He will keep His word and accomplish His will.

Sarah and Abraham told Hagar their plan, then they put their plan into action. It was a plan to bring God's miracle about by purely natural, human means. And the plan backfired.

There are many motivational speakers who host seminars, write books, and appear on TV, selling pseudospiritual self-help notions that are designed to bring about a "miracle" through purely human means. They give their ideas pleasant-sounding names—the power of positive thinking, new thought, positive mental attitude, positive affirmations, transcendental meditation, a course in miracles, the power of now, creative visualization, and so on. Some of these New Age gurus even throw in some Christian-sounding jargon to draw in gullible Christians, but there is nothing biblical about their teachings.

They can't teach you how to produce miracles. Only God can work a miracle. He is asking you and me to have faith and patience as we wait on Him. Whatever God has promised to us in His Word, He will do, and He doesn't need our help.

## God's Care for Hagar

When Hagar became pregnant, Sarah discovered the truth of the old adage, "Be careful what you wish for—you may get it." When Hagar realized she was pregnant, she began to despise Sarah—and Sarah turned right around and blamed Abraham:

> Sarai said to Abram, "You are responsible for the wrong I am suffering. I put my slave in your arms, and now that she knows she is pregnant, she despises me. May the LORD judge between you and me."
> "Your slave is in your hands," Abram said. "Do with her whatever you think best." Then Sarai mistreated Hagar; so she fled from her. (Gen. 16:5–6)

Sarah resented Hagar and proceeded to mistreat her. She verbally abused and berated Hagar and may have physically attacked her as well—anything to wipe that grin off Hagar's face. We only know for sure that Sarah mistreated Hagar in some way.

Notice how fickle Sarah's memory was. She angrily blamed Abraham for this mess. Now Hagar was pregnant, Sarah was despised, and it was all Abraham's fault. It's as if Sarah completely forgot that this entire scheme was her idea. Sarah's intentions may have been good—but as the old saying goes, "The road to hell is paved with good intentions." That is truer than most of us realize. Trouble always follows when we substitute good intentions for authentic obedience.

111

The Bible doesn't tell us how Abraham responded to Sarah's accusations. I picture him dodging flying crockery and stammering, "Sugar dumpling! Honey lamb! Remember, this was your idea."

And I can just see Sarah's eyes flashing, as she says, "My idea! Don't you try to pin this on me! You could have said no!"

What about poor Hagar? She thought that having the boss's baby would earn her a promotion, but it got her only punishment. The more her figure blossomed, the more cantankerous Sarah got. All Hagar did was follow orders.

But along with Hagar's undeserved troubles, she was about to receive unexpected blessings. Never underestimate God. He will give you unexpected blessings when you go through undeserved troubles. Our God is a God of justice, and He sees what is going on.

Hagar knew it was dangerous for her and her unborn child to remain in Abraham's household. The only thing she could do was run away. What happened when she ran away?

> The angel of the LORD found Hagar near a spring in the desert; it was the spring that is beside the road to Shur. And he said, "Hagar, slave of Sarai, where have you come from, and where are you going?"
>
> "I'm running away from my mistress Sarai," she answered.
>
> Then the angel of the LORD told her, "Go back to your mistress and submit to her." The angel added, "I will increase your descendants so much that they will be too numerous to count."
>
> The angel of the LORD also said to her:
>
>> "You are now pregnant
>> and you will give birth to a son.

112

You shall name him Ishmael,
    for the LORD has heard of your misery.
He will be a wild donkey of a man;
    his hand will be against everyone
        and everyone's hand against him,
and he will live in hostility
    toward all his brothers."

She gave this name to the LORD who spoke to her: "You are the God who sees me," for she said, "I have now seen the One who sees me." That is why the well was called Beer Lahai Roi; it is still there, between Kadesh and Bered.

So Hagar bore Abram a son, and Abram gave the name Ishmael to the son she had borne. Abram was eighty-six years old when Hagar bore him Ishmael. (Gen. 16:7–16)

This is the first time in Scripture we see the phrase "the angel of the LORD." This is no ordinary angel. I believe that this angel is nothing less than a theophany, an appearance of the preincarnate Lord Jesus Christ. (We previously saw a theophany in Abraham's encounter with Melchizedek, King of Salem, in Genesis 14.)

Jesus, the Son of God, was born as a human baby in Bethlehem more than two thousand years ago—but that was not the beginning of His existence. The Son of God was coexistent with God the Father from before the beginning of the world, as John describes Jesus in his Gospel: "Through him all things were made; without him nothing was made that has been made" (John 1:3). And Paul affirms this great truth about Jesus: "For in him all things were created: things in heaven and on earth, visible and invisible, whether thrones or powers or rulers or authorities; all things have been created through him and for him" (Col. 1:16).

When this angel appears to Hagar (the word *angel* means "messenger"), Hagar calls Him "Lord." The text tells us, "She gave this name to the Lord who spoke to her: 'You are the God who sees me,' for she said, 'I have now seen the One who sees me.'" Clearly, Hagar knew she had seen God in human form.

When Hagar despaired in the desert, believing she was abandoned and without hope, God came to her and gave her hope. Whenever you are tempted to think God has forsaken you, that He does not care about you and the trials you face, remember Hagar. Remember that she called Him "the God who sees me."

He is the God who sees you as well. He not only sees you, but He knows all the details of your life. He knows your hurts, your needs, your guilt, your longings. He knows you better than you know yourself.

## Be Patient with God's Delays

Have you ever tried to run away from the place of obedience? The Lord wants you to be patient and wait—but you run! I've tried running from obedience a couple of times in my life, and I only ended up miserable. I discovered that the place of blessing is in the place of obedience.

It has become an epidemic in our culture today—running from our problems instead of staying and facing them. Problems in the marriage? "I want a divorce." Problems in the workplace? "I quit." Problems at church? "I'll find a church that doesn't have problems." (Good luck with that.) When trouble comes our way, we run.

The problem with trying to run from our problems is that the real problem is within us. The problems in our marriage, our workplace, our church—at least half of every problem is our own doing. So when we run away, we take our problems with us. If we go into a new marriage, a new job, or a new church, we discover, "I didn't escape the problem! Here it is again!" Why? Because *the problem is us*. And we can't run away from ourselves.

But God seeks us out. He is present with us, even when we try to run away. As the psalmist writes, "If I rise on the wings of the dawn, if I settle on the far side of the sea, even there your hand will guide me, your right hand will hold me fast" (Ps. 139:9–10). That is the truth an Egyptian slave girl named Hagar discovered beside a spring in the desert.

Where was Hagar running to? She was probably going back to Egypt. It's a good thing God intercepted her before she went too far. There wasn't much call for pregnant unwed mothers in Egypt. She would only have been miserable there too.

It couldn't have been easy for Hagar to turn her steps back toward the camp of Abraham. When Hagar became pregnant, she began to despise Sarah—and Sarah despised her in return. Hagar had every reason to expect she would receive more mistreatment at the hands of her mistress. But Hagar obeyed the message from the Lord.

God had announced to Hagar that she was about to receive unexpected blessings. But to receive those blessings, she had to go back to the tent of Abraham and Sarah. She had to return to the path of obedience. The Bible makes it clear that the path of obedience is the path of blessing, but the path of disobedience leads to desolation.

In the early years of my walk with the Lord, I would cry to God when my problems became too great to bear: "God, please change my circumstances!" And God would let me pout and cry for a while. Finally, in a sweet, quiet voice, God would say, "Michael, before I change your circumstances, I want to change you."

And God had a similar message for Hagar. He said to her, in effect, "I will bless you, Hagar, but you need to go back to the place of obedience. You will have a son and you shall call his name Ishmael, which means 'God hears.' I have heard the cry of your affliction. I hear the cry of those who have been mistreated. I hear your cry, Hagar."

When God asked Hagar where she came from and where she was going, He wasn't asking for information He didn't possess. God already knew everything about her. He is omniscient. But He wanted her to verbalize her past pain and her despair about the future so that healing could begin.

I believe that when Hagar turned back, she was a changed woman. And not only that, but she also changed the heart of Abraham. She continued to live in Abraham's household for thirteen years.

In our desperation to change our circumstances, we often try to change them in our way and in our time. We impatiently stop trusting God and His plan for our lives, and we begin looking for a way around the crossing gate and flashing red lights God has placed in our paths for our protection. When we try to shortcut God's timetable for our lives, we inevitably find ourselves in the path of a locomotive. When we try to hurry God's plan, our impatience leads to disaster.

There are good reasons for God's delays. He is working on many fronts at the same time, preparing hearts, arranging events, and lining up circumstances. His blessing will be revealed. His purpose will be fulfilled. We just need to maintain a trusting faith. We need to pray, "Lord, I trust You. Lead me to the place of obedience. Take me to the place of blessing. I will wait for You to work Your miracle in my life."

# 7

# The Silence of God

Silence.

Some people crave it. Others detest it.

Some aren't happy unless they are surrounded by noise—they can't go anywhere without music blasting into their brains from a pair of earbuds. They can't even go to sleep without the TV or a streaming music device on. Silence makes them anxious and irritable.

Others are driven crazy by noise. Even the sound of cracking knuckles or slurping soup can cause great mental discomfort. There is a medical name for the kind of hypersensitivity to sound that drives some people into a rage: misophonia. Silence, for such people, is truly golden.

In a marriage relationship, silence isn't always golden. Silence can sometimes be more deafening and destructive than the noise of arguments. Between a husband and wife, silence often means isolation, bitterness, and a lack of communication.

Silence can also be deafening in our relationship with God. When we are silent, we have ceased to pray to God, we have stopped seeking fellowship with Him and guidance from Him. We have cut God out of our thoughts and plans. We are neither listening for His voice nor talking to Him.

But what about when God is silent? What about those times when we pray, but we do not hear God speaking to us? We easily misinterpret His silence. We think God has abandoned us. He has stopped answering our prayers. He has even stopped hearing our prayers. We think God is angry with us, and we blame Him for giving us the silent treatment.

Most Christians, at some point in their lives, experience the silence of God. I know I have. Many years ago, God was silent when I really needed Him to give me direction and guidance. So I prayed, "God, if I don't hear from You, I'll die!" I admit it—that was an exaggeration. At times, I can be a drama queen. But I really did have an intense desire to feel God's direction in my life, and I couldn't sense it at all.

Through that experience and others, I've learned a lot about the silences of God. I've learned that God often uses silence in our lives to speak to us in a new way and to accomplish His plan for our lives. Often, the silence of God is as meaningful as His voice. He sometimes uses silence for His redemptive purposes. When God is silent, we have an opportunity to discern the message hidden in His silence. But remember this: even when God is silent, He is working on our behalf.

## When God Is Silent

How can we learn to discern the meaning of the silences of God? I can think of no better way than by looking at specific events in Scripture when God was silent, events in which God's purpose for remaining silent became abundantly clear.

### The Silence of God's Judgment

In 1 Samuel 3, Eli the priest is in charge of the tabernacle. His sons are rebellious, corrupt, and disobedient. Eli has been so busy serving in the tabernacle that he has neglected his duties as a father. Because Eli has failed to discipline his two sons, God has stopped speaking to Eli. This is a sign of God's judgment against Eli for his failure as a father—yet Eli didn't understand why God had stopped speaking to him.

Eli was raising and mentoring a boy named Samuel. The boy's mother, Hannah, had dedicated Samuel to God and placed him in Eli's care. (The boy Samuel, of course, would grow up to become the prophet Samuel, who would anoint King Saul and King David.) One night, God called to Samuel, and the boy thought Eli had called him. When he went to Eli and said, "Here I am," Eli replied, "I did not call; go back and lie down" (v. 5).

This happened three times, and finally Eli realized that God wanted to speak to him through Samuel. He told Samuel to go back to bed and when he heard the voice again, he was to say, "Speak, Lord, for your servant is listening" (v. 9).

Samuel obeyed, and God gave a message to Samuel for Eli—a message of judgment for Eli's moral failure. The prophecy of God was later carried out, and Eli and his sons died as a result of God's judgment. But God first expressed His judgment against Eli through silence. He had ceased to speak to Eli directly. He would only speak through the boy Samuel.

We see the silence of judgment in the New Testament story of Jesus and the woman taken in adultery in John 8. The religious leaders brought a woman to Jesus and said, "This woman was caught in the act of adultery. In the Law Moses commanded us to stone such women. Now what do you say?" (vv. 4–5).

Jesus didn't answer. He bent down and wrote on the ground with His finger. The religious leaders kept haranguing Him, trying to get Him to break His silence. He continued to silently write in the dust of the ground. Some people think He was writing a list of the sins of the woman's accusers.

Finally, He said, "Let any one of you who is without sin be the first to throw a stone at her" (v. 7). And the woman's accusers melted away, shamed not only by His words but also by the silence of His judgment.

### The Silence of God's Mercy

At times, God exercises His mercy toward us by saying nothing to us. Sometimes He waits in silence for us to repent. He gives us time in silence to respond to the conviction of the Holy Spirit. He gives us time in silence to reflect on His amazing love and grace toward us.

We easily misinterpret God's silence as anger when He may simply be giving us time to respond to His mercy. Be grateful for His merciful silence. But at the same time, don't mistake God's silence for a toleration of sin. Repent now and restore a right relationship with God. As the apostle Peter writes, "The Lord is not slow in keeping his promise, as some understand slowness. Instead he is patient with you, not wanting anyone to perish, but everyone to come to repentance" (2 Pet. 3:9). God is patient, but He does not indulge our sins, and we dare not take His mercy for granted.

## The Silence of Testing

Job endured greater suffering than most of us will ever know. This man lost almost everything—his children, his wealth, his health, his friends, and his human dignity. He was in extreme and constant pain. He was reduced to scraping the boils and sores of his skin with broken shards of pottery. His friends turned on him and falsely accused this innocent man of hidden sin.

When people think they have it rough, all they have to do is read the book of Job—and suddenly they have a new perspective on their problems. They're glad they have the problems they have and are not suffering the trials of Job. He endured emotional, spiritual, and physical suffering. He endured grief and humiliation, opposition and condemnation. But I submit to you that Job's greatest suffering resulted from the silence of God. Job poured out his anguished questions to God, but the sky was like a curtain of lead. Job received no answers from God.

The silence of God in the book of Job was due to God's testing of Job. By maintaining his faith and obedience to God in spite of God's silence, Job demonstrated before Satan and the fallen angels that God's judgment against them was just. If a mere flesh-and-blood man like Job could remain obedient in the face of so much suffering and the silence of God, then the rebellious angels who had seen God face-to-face were without excuse.

Job persisted in prayer in spite of God's silence. He was like the widow Jesus spoke of in one of His parables. She kept pounding on the door of the unjust judge, demanding that he listen to her and give her justice.[1] Sometimes God wants us to demonstrate that we will persist in trusting Him, in spite of His silence. We need to keep pounding on the door of heaven through our prayers. Don't give up. Unlike the unjust judge, God is more than willing to give us good gifts. Keep persevering in prayer.

### The Silence of Waiting

Sometimes God remains silent until we become quiet. When we are busy, noisy, and running off at the mouth, we can't hear God speak. Sometimes He waits for us to calm down so that He can do His work in our lives.

There's a difference between persevering (the silence of testing) and ceasing to strive (the silence of waiting). The difference between persevering and being still is our attitude. When we are tested but persevere in prayer, maintaining an absolute and unshakeable faith that God will answer, that is the silence of testing. We see this in the story of the Canaanite woman who repeatedly begged Jesus to heal her daughter in Matthew 15. First, Jesus was silent; then He kept changing the subject. Every time Jesus tried to distract her, she came right back to persevering in prayer for her daughter. Finally, Jesus said, "Woman, you have great faith! Your request is granted" (v. 28). And the woman's daughter was instantly healed.

There are times when God wants us to hammer away at the gates of heaven like this woman. But there are other times when He wants us to quiet our thoughts, let go of our anxious emotions, and be still in His presence before He speaks. This is the silence of waiting. As we read in Psalm 37:7:

> Be still before the LORD
> and wait patiently for him.

When God is silent, we need to pray for wisdom to know whether He wants us to storm the gates of heaven with our prayers or cease our striving and simply sit quietly in His presence, listening intently for His voice.

### The Silence of God's Love

Sometimes words distract from God's message. God doesn't merely want to instruct us. He also wants to embrace us with His love. We need to learn to rest, quietly and serenely, in His love. This is why He is sometimes silent. He is inviting us into His warm embrace. No words are needed. Words can't express what God feels for us and what we feel for God. He sent His Son to die for us. He forgave us, saved us, and redeemed us for all eternity. Now He wants us to rest in His love.

Are you listening to the silence of God? Are you sensing His love in the stillness all around you? Listen . . . listen . . . Do you hear that? It's the sound of God's heartbeat. His silence is the sound of His love.

## Thirteen Years of Silence

In Genesis 17, we find that God has been silent for thirteen years. Abraham was eighty-six years old at the end of Genesis 16; in Genesis 17, he is ninety-nine. What happened in

Abraham's life during those thirteen years between Genesis 16 and 17? We don't know. The Scriptures are silent—thirteen years of silence.

What was God doing in the lives of Abraham and Sarah during those thirteen silent years? Maybe God was giving Abraham and Sarah time to reflect on their sin of trying to rush God's plan. Or maybe God wanted to be sure that Abraham was so old, his seed so dead, that when Isaac, the son of promise, was finally born, God alone would receive the credit and glory for his miraculous conception and birth. Or maybe the answer is simply that nothing of importance happened during those years.

At the end of Genesis 16, Hagar was returning to live with Abraham and Sarah. In Genesis 17, Hagar is a changed woman, living in the household of Abraham and Sarah. God has changed the hearts of Abraham and Sarah, and they now accept her as part of their home.

Perhaps Abraham thought that everything was going well in his life. He had a son and thought that all the blessings God had promised him would be bestowed on Ishmael, and that was just fine with Abraham. But after thirteen uneventful years, God was about to shake Abraham out of his comfort zone.

One of the most common misconceptions believers have about the Christian life is that a problem-free, uneventful life means that all is well in our relationship with the Lord. According to this view, trials, obstacles, and opposition mean that God is angry and there are problems in our relationship with the Lord. While it's true that God does sometimes use crises and trials to get our attention, this is not always the case. Smooth sailing through life doesn't necessarily mean there is smooth sailing in our relationship with God.

I believe Abraham had grown complacent during those thirteen silent years. He had ceased to count stars when he could see no stars. In fact, I believe he thought that his son by Hagar, Ishmael, was one of those stars. He apparently stopped believing that God had promised him a son by his wife Sarah. He had begun to place his future hopes on Ishmael. In Genesis 17:18, we see Abraham tell God, "If only Ishmael might live under your blessing!" Abraham had decided to settle for Ishmael instead of waiting for the son God had promised him. He had decided that Ishmael would do.

But God would not let Abraham give up on His promise. God was about to rock Abraham's world. He was going to prove to Abraham, on no uncertain terms, that Sarah—not Hagar the Egyptian slave—was the woman through whom His promise would be fulfilled. Sarah was the one who would be the progenitor of God's Messiah.

Throughout the four thousand years of Jewish history, various kings and nations have tried to eliminate God's chosen people. Horrible acts of mass murder have been committed against them, but God has always protected a remnant of His people. God's chosen people, the Jews, have gone through enslavement, exile, pogroms, diasporas, and the Holocaust. Satan could read the biblical prophecies of the Messiah, and he did his best to destroy the people of the Messiah, the lineage of the Messiah, and the Messiah Himself.

The promise God made to Abraham was ultimately the promise of the coming Messiah—and God was going to fulfill His plan through the free woman, Sarah, not the Egyptian slave woman, Hagar. God had a plan for the salvation of the human race through Abraham's seed, the Messiah,

Jesus. Abraham had unwittingly circumvented God's plan by going outside of his marriage in the attempt to conceive a son by Hagar. By his disobedience, Abraham posed a threat to the very promise God had made to him.

So God had to shake Abraham out of his satisfaction with Ishmael. He had to reorient Abraham to the powerful truths of His covenant. God had to show Abraham that He was going to fulfill His promises with absolute precision—and He was going to fulfill them through Sarah, not Hagar. God answers prayer and He fulfills His promises.

### "I Will" and "You Must"

When Abraham was ninety-nine years old, the Lord appeared to him. Let's look at the opening verses of Genesis 17:

> When Abram was ninety-nine years old, the LORD appeared to him and said, "I am God Almighty; walk before me faithfully and be blameless. Then I will make my covenant between me and you and will greatly increase your numbers."
>
> Abram fell facedown, and God said to him, "As for me, this is my covenant with you: You will be the father of many nations. No longer will you be called Abram; your name will be Abraham, for I have made you a father of many nations. I will make you very fruitful; I will make nations of you, and kings will come from you. I will establish my covenant as an everlasting covenant between me and you and your descendants after you for the generations to come, to be your God and the God of your descendants after you. The whole land of Canaan, where you now reside as a foreigner, I will give as an everlasting possession to you and your descendants after you; and I will be their God."

Then God said to Abraham, "As for you, you must keep my covenant, you and your descendants after you for the generations to come." (vv. 1–9)

This is the first time God identified Himself as *El Shaddai*, the God of power and might (translated "God Almighty" in v. 1). What is God saying to Abraham? Why does He identify Himself with that name? He is saying, in effect, "Abraham, I don't need you to improvise on My plan. I only need your obedience. I don't need you to accelerate My timetable. Just obey My word. I am capable of fulfilling all My promises. All I need from you, Abraham, is your faith and your obedience. It's time for you to start counting stars again, whether you see them or not."

This passage raises some questions: If God demands Abraham's obedience, is His covenant truly unilateral? If God's promise is unilateral, can't He do it all by Himself, whether Abraham obeys or not?

Let's extend these questions even further to the unilateral covenant God has made with us, the new covenant of Christ's blood. Can salvation take place without our co-operation with God? Please pay close attention to the answer to all these questions.

On the one hand, our God is a sovereign God. He's the God who is in absolute control. One of my life verses is Ephesians 1:11—"In him we were also chosen, having been predestined according to the plan of him who works out everything in conformity with the purpose of his will." God accomplishes all things according to the counsel of His will.

On the other hand, God demands our response. In this passage, God says "I will" again and again: "*I will* make you very fruitful; *I will* make nations of you. . . . *I will* establish my covenant as an everlasting covenant. . . . *I will* give [the land of Canaan] as an everlasting possession to you and your descendants after you; and *I will* be their God."

But there is a contrast to the Lord's "I will" statements. Later in this passage, God tells Abraham that in response to this covenant, "you will" do this and "you must" do that. There are many lazy Christians who interpret the doctrine of the sovereignty of God to mean that they don't have to do anything—God will do it all. That is a false understanding of God's sovereignty.

When God says to Abraham "you must," He is not saying that His covenant depends on Abraham's action. The covenant depends on God's grace, period. But at the same time, the grace of God compels us to respond. Today, in New Testament times, when God saves us, He regenerates us. Don't let anybody tell you that your human spirit was in a coma or half asleep or taking a nap. The Bible says it was dead, dead, dead.

The Holy Spirit has to come in and raise us up. He changes our hearts. When the Holy Spirit convicts us, we are able to say, "O Lord, I am a sinner, headed for hell. Save me, forgive me!" And we respond to His love. He regenerates us, then He justifies us. If grace does not make us different from other human beings, it is not truly the grace of God.

If you are not living for God, if you are not loving God, if you are not obeying the Word of God, it could be an indication that you have never been regenerated by God. In fact, your obedience and your love for God and His Word are the only evidence that you have become a born-again believer. If you have never been regenerated, if the Lord Jesus is speaking to you, saying, "I want to bring you to Myself. I want you to believe in Me and be saved," I hope, right here and now, you will respond: "Here I am, Lord. I repent of my sins, and I turn to You for my salvation."

Don't waste another moment of your life living for yourself. Turn to Him, receive Him, and live for Him.

## God's Best—or Second Best?

In Genesis 17, God changed Abram's name to Abraham, from exalted father to father of a multitude. Please understand: Abraham's obedience did not contribute anything to the covenant. In fact, the opposite is true. In the next few verses, God institutes the ritual of circumcision, the cutting away of the male flesh. This ritual signifies the renouncing of human effort, the work of the flesh.

In many ways, the Lord's Supper is like this. It is our testimony to the world that we believe we cannot save ourselves. We can only be saved through the shed blood of Jesus on the cross two thousand years ago. We are testifying to the world that we cannot live this life without God's strength. At the Lord's Table, we declare our dependence on Jesus. We declare that we cannot go to heaven apart from the shed blood of Jesus Christ. We cannot partake in the marriage supper of the Lamb without the shed blood of Jesus Christ.

The key to Genesis 17 is verse 1, in which God tells Abraham, "I am God Almighty [*El Shaddai*]; walk before me faithfully and be blameless." What does this mean? It means that we are to trust in His Word implicitly. We are to trust in His promises unconditionally. We are to trust in His plan completely. We are to stop trying to improve on God's plan.

God goes on to say, "Then I will make my covenant between me and you and will greatly increase your numbers." And God lists many other things He will do for Abraham and his descendants. Then He lists the things Abraham and his descendants must do in return, including the rite of circumcision. And finally, God says this concerning Abraham's wife Sarah:

> As for Sarai your wife, you are no longer to call her Sarai; her name will be Sarah. I will bless her and will surely give you a son by her. I will bless her so that she will be the mother of nations; kings of peoples will come from her. (vv. 15–16)

Sarah's original name, Sarai, which was given to her in Mesopotamia, means "contentious one" or "she who strives." But when God reconfirms His promise of a son by her, He tells Abraham that henceforth he is to call her *Sarah*, which means "princess." Why? Because, God explains, "she will be the mother of nations; kings of peoples will come from her."

And what is Abraham's response to God's promise concerning Sarah? Laughter, disbelief, and a strange lack of gratitude: "Abraham fell facedown; he laughed and said to himself, 'Will a son be born to a man a hundred years old? Will Sarah bear a child at the age of ninety?' And Abraham said to God, 'If only Ishmael might live under your blessing!'" (vv. 17–18).

Isn't that amazing? God has just promised blessing upon blessing to Abraham and his descendants—and to top it all off, He has promised to open Sarah's womb and give Abraham the son of the promise, a son born not to an Egyptian slave but to Abraham's own freeborn wife. And Abraham

132

laughs and says, "If only Ishmael might live under your blessing!" In other words, "Ishmael will do. Just bless him. He's already here. Just use the boy we already have. Don't go to the trouble of causing Sarah to have a baby."

Have you ever experienced the frustration of trying to explain an important idea to someone, and that person just doesn't get it? In fact, that person *refuses* to understand what you are saying? Isn't that exasperating? Doesn't that try your patience? That's how God must have felt as He tried to get Abraham to understand the importance of the promise He was making to him. God, in His infinite patience, chose to explain His plan to Abraham one more time:

> Then God said, "Yes, but your wife Sarah will bear you a son, and you will call him Isaac. I will establish my covenant with him as an everlasting covenant for his descendants after him. And as for Ishmael, I have heard you: I will surely bless him; I will make him fruitful and will greatly increase his numbers. He will be the father of twelve rulers, and I will make him into a great nation. But my covenant I will establish with Isaac, whom Sarah will bear to you by this time next year." When he had finished speaking with Abraham, God went up from him. (vv. 19–22)

In other words, "Abraham, I'll explain it to you one more time, even though I've been trying to tell you this for the last thirty years. I am El Shaddai, almighty God, for whom nothing is impossible. I am the God who created the stars and galaxies with a word. I am the God who ordains the times and the seasons, the daytime and the nighttime, the sunshine and the rains. I will bless Ishmael greatly, but I am establishing my covenant with a son who will be born to Sarah next year. When he is born, you will name him Isaac, 'He Laughs'—a reminder of your response today to the promise I made to you. I want you to always remember, whenever you call Isaac by name, that I am the God who keeps His promises and works miracles in your life, even after you have laughed at that promise."

Abraham finally gets it. God is going to give him a son through Sarah—and for the first time, God has given him a timeframe: "by this time next year." Abraham doesn't understand the prophetic ramifications of God's promise to him. He doesn't understand that God plans to bring forth the Messiah, the Son of God, through Abraham's line of descendants. He doesn't know that God plans to send His Son, the descendant of Abraham, Isaac, and Jacob, of the house of David, to earth to be born as a baby and to die on a cross, and that this Son will become the Lord and Savior of all who believe in Him.

Abraham couldn't possibly understand the truth that the apostle Paul will explain in a letter to the Galatians some two thousand years later: "The promises were spoken to Abraham and to his seed. Scripture does not say 'and to seeds,' meaning many people, but 'and to your seed,' meaning one person, who is Christ" (Gal. 3:16). God was offering Abraham and the entire human race His very best—the plan of salvation by grace through faith in Jesus Christ. Yet Abraham was more than willing to settle for second best—Ishmael will do.

How often do you and I settle for second best when God longs to give us His best? How often have we settled when God says, "I have an amazing future planned for you"? God wants us to know: "I have new territories for you to conquer in My name, new and exciting opportunities for you to serve in My kingdom. There are many souls you can win for Me, so many new ministries to be accomplished."

Friend in Christ, I plead with you: don't settle for second best in your Christian walk; don't settle for anything less than God's very best.

## When Silence Speaks Louder Than Words

God said to Abraham, in effect, "I'm going to bless you, and I'm going to bless the world through you." He blesses us individually as believers so that we will be a blessing to others. He doesn't bless us so that we can form a Bless Me Club. He doesn't bless us so that we can be rich and warm and filled while the rest of the world goes to hell. No, we are to use the blessings God showers on us to bless others, to serve others, to save others.

Do God's blessings flow freely through you to others? Or are you hoarding God's blessings the way Ebenezer Scrooge hoarded gold? You have been blessed with the good news of Jesus Christ. You have been forgiven, redeemed, and saved. Do you share the blessings of the good news with others? Do you share your Christian testimony with others? Do you tell others how to know Christ as Lord and Savior? Do you tell others how they too can be forgiven, redeemed, and saved?

If you are not experiencing the overwhelming blessings of God, it might be that you have been grasping God's blessings so tightly that you have been choking them to death. The flow of God's blessings often stops altogether when they are grasped too tightly. Open your hands. Release God's blessings to the people around you—and prepare to be amazed as God pours a flood of blessings through your life and onto the people around you.

God finally got His message through to Abraham—then God left him. What did Abraham do? The concluding verses of Genesis 17 tell us:

> On that very day Abraham took his son Ishmael and all those born in his household or bought with his money, every male in his household, and circumcised them, as God told him. Abraham was ninety-nine years old when he was circumcised, and his son Ishmael was thirteen; Abraham and his son Ishmael were both circumcised on that very day. And every male in Abraham's household, including those born in his household or bought from a foreigner, was circumcised with him. (vv. 23–27)

God gave Abraham the rite of circumcision to carry out as a sign of obedience. How did Abraham respond? He didn't say, "Okay, Lord, I'll do that circumcision thing you mentioned real soon—maybe next week. Or next month, when I have more time. When I get around to it." No, Genesis tells us that Abraham obeyed immediately. Twice, the text says that Abraham carried out God's command "on that very day."

Though Abraham was slow to grasp God's promise, though he tried in his ignorance and impatience to change the terms of God's promise, once God finally got through to him, Abraham obeyed. After thirteen years of silence, God spoke—and Abraham finally understood.

If you've ever been in a classroom of noisy children, you may have seen the teacher try to get the children's attention by calling to them or shouting to them, all to no avail. What works? Often the only thing that gets through to noisy children is silence. The teacher will stand and wait, saying nothing—and gradually the classroom will come to order. Sometimes silence speaks louder than words.

Are you experiencing the silence of God right now? Perhaps God wants to move you out of your comfort zone, your complacency. Perhaps He has tried to explain His plan for your life, and you have not been listening. Perhaps His silence is a meaningful silence. Listen to the message of the silence of God.

Then respond to Him. Obey Him. Receive the blessings He wants to shower on you—and share His blessings with the world.

# 8

# The Friend of God

The older I get, the more I cherish genuine friendship.

What is a friend? A true friend is a person who moves deeper into your life when everyone else is leaving. A true friend loves you with all of your quirks and idiosyncrasies. A true friend knows everything about you and loves you anyway.

In the Middle East, we have a saying about friendship. It rhymes in the original language, but in English it goes like this: "Your enemy will count to you every one of your faults, but your friends will even swallow gravel for you." This is a vivid description of true friendship.

Genesis 18 reveals a priceless dimension of the relationship between Abraham and the Lord. You cannot place a value on it: Abraham becomes God's friend.

You might ask, "Isn't everybody a friend of God?" No, not really. But we can be. How can we, weak and sinful human beings, become friends to a righteous and holy God?

The basis of friendship with God is faith. It is faith that connects us to Him. It is faith that enabled Abraham to be God's friend. Even with all his failures, Abraham became God's friend because of his faith. Despite his weakness, failure, and sin, Abraham had great faith in God.

It was faith that made King David a friend of God. The Lord saw David as a man after His own heart. Why? It was certainly not because David was perfect. During one extremely low point in his life, David committed adultery, murder, and a bigger cover-up than Watergate. David was a flawed human being, but he was a friend of God because he had great faith in God.

Faith enabled Enoch to not only walk with God but also enter heaven without passing through death.[1] The Scriptures tell us very little about this ancient man, but from what we do know, it is clear that Enoch, like Abraham and David, was a friend of God.

When you and I were lost in sin, God extended His friendship to us. He gave us His one and only Son, Jesus, to die on the cross and rise again to bring us together as friends. That's why choosing Jesus above all else, loving Jesus above everyone else, pleasing Jesus before anyone else, spending unhurried time with Jesus before anything else, delighting in the presence and companionship of Jesus beyond all else, and proclaiming Jesus unashamedly are proofs that we are a friend of God.

Genesis 18 is a remarkable passage of Scripture because it contains every aspect of what it means to be a friend of God—yet the word *friend* does not appear anywhere in the chapter. Abraham is called God's friend three times in the Bible, but not in Genesis 18, even though this chapter contains all the evidence of Abraham's friendship with God.

Abraham is first called God's friend in 2 Chronicles 20. In this passage, the nation of Israel is being threatened by powerful enemies, the Moabites and the Ammonites. The nation is in terrible danger. So Jehoshaphat stands in the temple and prays, "Our God, did you not drive out the inhabitants of this land before your people Israel and give it forever to the descendants of Abraham your friend?" (v. 7).

In the New Testament, the apostle James writes, "And the scripture was fulfilled that says, 'Abraham believed God, and it was credited to him as righteousness,' and he was called God's friend" (James 2:23).

But the most powerful and profound verse that speaks of Abraham as God's friend is Isaiah 41:8, where God Himself declares:

> But you, Israel, my servant,
> Jacob, whom I have chosen,
> you descendants of Abraham my friend.

Wouldn't you like God to call you "my friend"?

## God Knows Us Better Than We Know Ourselves

The story of Genesis 18 takes place very soon—probably days or weeks—after the events of Genesis 17. In obedience to God, Abraham had circumcised all the men and boys of his household, including the servants. Then the Lord comes to the camp of Abraham in the form of three visitors.

> The LORD appeared to Abraham near the great trees of Mamre while he was sitting at the entrance to his tent in the heat of the day. Abraham looked up and saw three men

standing nearby. When he saw them, he hurried from the entrance of his tent to meet them and bowed low to the ground.

He said, "If I have found favor in your eyes, my lord, do not pass your servant by. Let a little water be brought, and then you may all wash your feet and rest under this tree. Let me get you something to eat, so you can be refreshed and then go on your way—now that you have come to your servant."

"Very well," they answered, "do as you say."

So Abraham hurried into the tent to Sarah. "Quick," he said, "get three seahs of the finest flour and knead it and bake some bread."

Then he ran to the herd and selected a choice, tender calf and gave it to a servant, who hurried to prepare it. He then brought some curds and milk and the calf that had been prepared, and set these before them. While they ate, he stood near them under a tree. (Gen. 18:1–8)

As Abraham sits at the entrance to his tent, he sees the Lord, appearing in the form of three men. God does not appear to Abraham in a dream. He does not materialize before Abraham as El Shaddai. Instead, Abraham sees the preincarnate Christ. Abraham instantly knows that these are not ordinary visitors. In an act of worship, Abraham bows down at the feet of the preincarnate Christ and says, "If I have found favor in your eyes, my lord, do not pass your servant by. . . . Let me get you something to eat."

Here we see how much Abraham longed for the Lord's companionship. Notice how he rushes to meet the three visitors. He bows low and worships, then he immediately runs to provide the best food and comforts for his visitors. Worshiping and sacrificial giving are two sides of the same coin. Abraham didn't just go through the motions of worshiping the Lord. He sacrificed and served the Lord, treating Him as an honored guest.

Ever since God's first appearance to Abraham in Ur of the Chaldeans, He has been a friend to Abraham. God told Abraham to leave his country, his family, everything that was familiar to him, and go to a land Abraham didn't know, a land God would show to him and give to him. From that moment on, God did not deprive Abraham of His friendship and companionship. God walked with Abraham.

Now the Lord appears to Abraham in human form and sits with him. He arrives as a guest and shares a meal with Abraham. What a beautiful picture of friendship.

Think of all the times Abraham has wandered away from his friendship with the Lord. Remember how he drifted down into Egypt and lied and swindled Pharaoh? Remember how he tried to rush God's plan by having a baby with Sarah's slave girl? Yet God did not let those betrayals stop Him from pursuing His friendship with Abraham.

If you have wandered away from God, please know this, on the authority of God's Word: God is eager and ready to restore His friendship with you. He wants to deepen His friendship with you. He is longing for you to be in close communication and fellowship with Him.

The fact is friends talk to each other. Friends share thoughts with each other. Friends spend time together. Friends enjoy each other's company. Friends confide in each other. This is true even when one friend is God and the other is a mere human being.

Many people want friendship with God, but they don't want to come clean with God. They aren't willing to confess their sins, failings, and needs to Him. They try to hide a part of themselves from Him. But God is the best kind of friend you could ever have. He is the God who listens to our confession, who has compassion for our failures and needs, who offers forgiveness for our sins, and who can be trusted to keep our confidences.

Years ago, *Psychology Today* conducted a survey of forty thousand readers. The survey asked what they cherished most in a friendship. The answers might surprise you. Respondents named the fifth most important quality in a friendship as honesty and frankness (73 percent). The fourth most important quality was supportiveness (75 percent). The third most important quality was warmth and affection (82 percent). The second most important quality was loyalty (88 percent). And the most important quality of all in a friendship was the ability to keep confidences (89 percent of respondents).[2]

God is a friend who keeps confidences. He is also loyal, loving, supportive, and honest. God has all the qualities you are looking for in a friend. Above all, God knows us better than we know ourselves, as the next few verses in Genesis 18 show:

"Where is your wife Sarah?" they asked him.

"There, in the tent," he said.

Then one of them said, "I will surely return to you about this time next year, and Sarah your wife will have a son."

Now Sarah was listening at the entrance to the tent, which was behind him. Abraham and Sarah were already very old, and Sarah was past the age of childbearing. So Sarah laughed to herself as she thought, "After I am worn out and my lord is old, will I now have this pleasure?"

Then the LORD said to Abraham, "Why did Sarah laugh and say, 'Will I really have a child, now that I am old?' Is anything too hard for the LORD? I will return to you at the appointed time next year, and Sarah will have a son."

Sarah was afraid, so she lied and said, "I did not laugh." But he said, "Yes, you did laugh." (vv. 9–15)

God knew Abraham and Sarah through and through. They couldn't hide anything from Him. It was useless to lie to Him.

## Is Anything Too Hard for the Lord?

When the three visitors arrived and Abraham told Sarah to prepare food for them, she responded in gracious unity with her husband. She wanted to honor the Lord. No wonder the apostle Peter praises Sarah as an example of godly faith:

> For this is the way the holy women of the past who put their hope in God used to adorn themselves. They submitted themselves to their own husbands, like Sarah, who obeyed Abraham and called him her lord. You are her daughters if you do what is right and do not give way to fear. (1 Pet. 3:5–6)

To be sure, Sarah was far from perfect. But she was a woman of faith and character. Notice that the Lord asked for her by name: "Where is your wife Sarah?" Let's not pass over this too lightly. God knows us by name as well. He doesn't say, "Hey, you over there." He calls us by name. In the Gospels, Jesus called Nathaniel by name to be His disciple. He called Zacchaeus the tax collector by name and told him to come down from the tree. He called Saul of Tarsus by name on the road to Damascus. And He called you by name to be His follower. He knows you by name, and He loves you by name.

In Genesis 18:10, God repeats His promise of a son who will be born to Sarah: "I will surely return to you about this time next year, and Sarah your wife will have a son." You may wonder why God repeats this promise here, the very same promise He gave Abraham in Genesis 17:21: "But my covenant I will establish with Isaac, whom Sarah will bear to you by this time next year." Again, God does not waste words. The reason the Lord repeats this promise is that Sarah wasn't present when He spoke it in Genesis 17. He repeats it in Genesis 18 so that she can hear the promise with her own ears.

But didn't Abraham tell Sarah about the promise after God told him in Genesis 17? No, he didn't. How do we know? We know Abraham didn't tell her because of what happens in Genesis 18. Sarah was eavesdropping from the side of the tent (and the Lord, of course, knew she was hidden there). The Lord repeated His promise to make sure Sarah heard it—and when she heard the Lord say she would have a baby within a year, she was so shocked and startled that she laughed out loud. If Abraham had told her what the Lord had said in Genesis 17, Sarah would not have been so shocked. (Perhaps Abraham kept the Lord's promise to himself because he didn't think Sarah's aged heart could stand the strain!)

Isn't this like our Lord? He made a special trip to Abraham's encampment so that He could personally tell Sarah the news. In verse 12, Sarah thought, "After I am worn out and my lord is old, will I now have this pleasure?" She just couldn't fathom that a ninety-year-old woman could have a baby.

From a human point of view, her reaction is understandable. No wonder Abraham was reluctant to tell her! He's a ninety-nine-year-old man looking at his ninety-year-old wife, imagining how to break the news to her: "Sugar dumpling, you know what? Um, we're going to have a baby. That's right. You're going to get pregnant, have morning sickness, get big, and deliver the baby in the usual way. No, Honey lamb, I'm not crazy. God Himself told me." After rehearsing his speech a few times, Abraham took the coward's way out and said nothing.

So God made a return visit and repeated His promise to Abraham, knowing that Sarah was hiding in the shadows, eavesdropping. She overheard—and she laughed.

It's interesting that the Lord didn't ask Sarah why she laughed. Instead, He asked Abraham, "Why did Sarah laugh?" I have a theory (it doesn't have the authority of Scripture, but this is what I believe) that when the Lord said, "Why did Sarah laugh?" it was a rebuke to Abraham. The Lord was saying indirectly, "Why is Sarah surprised by this news? Why didn't you tell her about My promise?"

The Lord quickly adds, in one of my favorite verses in the Bible, "Is anything too hard for the LORD?" It's a rhetorical question—a question that answers itself: no, nothing is too hard for the Lord!

I have seen many Christians who seem to have lost faith in the power of God. They think that maybe there are some problems and challenges that are too hard for the Lord. The culture war against Christians in our society—too hard for the Lord! The battle against abortion—too hard for the Lord! My financial problems—too hard for the Lord! The problems in my marriage—too hard for the Lord! I see believers walking around looking lost, hopeless, and defeated. It's as if they were baptized in vinegar and weaned on lemon juice. We need to remind ourselves of the promise of God. Is anything too hard for the Lord? No!

I believe many of us think that some things are too hard for the Lord because we have not been praying about them or we have not been praying with right motives. The apostle James tells us, "When you ask, you do not receive, because you ask with wrong motives, that you may spend what you get on your pleasures" (James 4:3). Let's not blame the Lord for our own failure to pray with right motives.

Is anything too hard for the Lord? No! This refrain resounds throughout Scripture. In Numbers 11:23, God asks Moses if the power of God is limited. Answer: No! In Jeremiah 32:17, the prophet looks to God and says, "Ah, Sovereign LORD, you have made the heavens and the earth by your great power and outstretched arm. Nothing is too hard for you."

In Luke 1, the angel Gabriel tells Mary that she is going to have a child, and Mary asks how that's possible since she is a virgin. The angel says, "No word from God will ever fail" (v. 37). In other words, nothing is too hard for the Lord.

If we honestly, intensely, and authentically believed these words, we would have churches packed to the rafters, not only on Sunday mornings but also at midweek prayer meetings and every other time the church doors are open. Genuine faith makes the church more powerful, vital, and effective. Unbelief leads to churches and Christians who are spiritually lifeless and sin-ridden.

There's nothing wrong with experiencing doubt from time to time. We all go through times of doubt. In John 8, Jesus gives us the solution to doubt when He says, "If you hold to my teaching, you are really my disciples. Then you will know the truth, and the truth will set you free" (vv. 31–32). In times of doubt, hold to the Lord's teachings, obey His commandments, and follow His leading in spite of your doubts and questions. If you hold to His teachings and continue living like a disciple of the Lord, you will know the truth, and the truth will set you free from your doubts.

It's not a sin to doubt. But it can become a sin if we remain in our doubts to the point at which doubt hardens into unbelief, and unbelief produces sin. That's what happened to Sarah.

The Lord said she was going to have a baby within the year. Her response was laughter—the laughter of unbelief. But her sin didn't stop there. One sin always leads to another. In this case, the sin of unbelief led to the sin of lying to God. The Lord asked Abraham, "Why did Sarah laugh?"

Sarah lied and said, "I did not laugh."

And the Lord said, "Yes, you did laugh."

While it's true that Sarah experienced unbelief at this point and tried to cover it up with a lie, it was as a result of this very encounter with the Lord that Sarah became a great woman of faith. Hebrews 11 declares, "And by faith even Sarah, who was past childbearing age, was enabled to bear children because she considered him faithful who had made the promise" (v. 11).

After Sarah's laughter, after her lie, after her failure of faith, she learned that the word of the Lord could be trusted, no matter how late it was in coming, no matter how improbable or impossible it seemed to be. In months to come, as a new life was conceived and began growing in Sarah's womb—a womb she had thought was dead and incapable of conceiving a child—she learned that nothing, absolutely *nothing*, is too hard for the Lord.

Finally, the blessed day came. Baby Isaac was about to be born. As Sarah went into labor, I imagine that with every contraction, no matter how painful, she praised God for the miraculous gift of being a mother at last.

Nothing is too hard for the Lord!

## When God Says, "Enough!"

In Genesis 18:16–33, we see a beautiful picture of Abraham walking with the Lord, communing with the Lord, and fellowshiping with the Lord. But the key verse in this passage regarding friendship with God is verse 17: "Then the LORD said, 'Shall I hide from Abraham what I am about to do?'" As we are about to see, God explicitly demonstrated His friendship with Abraham in a powerful way.

Friends confide in one another. Even though God is God and man is man, God confides in Abraham. He says: "Shall I hide from Abraham what I am about to do?" God will not hide His plans from His friend Abraham. This is evidence that proves the depth of their friendship. As the psalmist writes:

> The LORD confides in those who fear him;
> he makes his covenant known to them. (Ps. 25:14)

And the prophet Amos concurs:

> Surely the Sovereign LORD does nothing
> without revealing his plan
> to his servants the prophets. (Amos 3:7)

At this point, we have to take note of the great strides Abraham has made in his character and spiritual maturity. We have seen him in Egypt, fearful, lying, and conniving. We have seen him yielding to Sarah's urging that he father a son in an attempt to hurry God's plan. We have seen him willing to settle for second best, urging God to carry out His plan through Ishmael, the son of a slave girl, instead of the son God had promised.

And thank God that the Bible shows Abraham and Sarah to us in "high definition" so that we can see they are not plastic saints but real human beings. They sin, they fail, they lose faith. They are the kind of real, flawed human beings whom you and I can identify with.

The good news is that the character and faith of Abraham and Sarah are not static. Both of these heroes of the faith change and grow and reach new levels of spiritual maturity. This means that you and I can change and grow and mature in Christ as well. Abraham has come a long way, and so can we.

God is about to tell His friend Abraham about His plans for the wicked cities of Sodom and Gomorrah.

> "Abraham will surely become a great and powerful nation, and all nations on earth will be blessed through him. For I have chosen him, so that he will direct his children and his household after him to keep the way of the LORD by doing what is right and just, so that the LORD will bring about for Abraham what he has promised him."
>
> Then the LORD said, "The outcry against Sodom and Gomorrah is so great and their sin so grievous that I will go down and see if what they have done is as bad as the outcry that has reached me. If not, I will know." (Gen. 18:18–21)

151

The Lord takes Abraham into His confidence, as if to say, "Abraham, my friend, there is a disaster looming on the horizon—and it's in your backyard. The cities of Sodom and Gomorrah have become cesspools of sin and violence. The cup of iniquity is full to the brim. My patience has run out, and I will soon send My judgment raining down on those cities."

If God was ready to judge Sodom and Gomorrah for the sins rampant in those cities, how will our own civilization escape God's judgment? Read the first chapter of Romans and see if our own society doesn't fall under the condemnation of God's righteous judgment. I have no doubt that the Lord is saying to us today, "My patience is running out. The nation that once honored Me now despises Me. The nation that was once a city on a hill now provokes Me with its abominations. The nation from whose pulpits the gospel once rang out around the world is now preaching falsehoods. The nation that once took the gospel to the ends of the earth has become self-centered and drunk on self-worship."

God's cup of wrath and judgment is already overflowing. I am convinced that God's judgment has already begun. Many believers are totally oblivious to it. It's not too late to repent and return, but the time is fast approaching when God will say, "Enough," and He will leave us to the consequences of our choices.

Abraham was horrified to hear God's plans. His nephew Lot lived in Sodom. If God destroyed Sodom, Lot and his entire family would die along with the wicked. So Abraham pleads with God for the righteous people in Sodom:

> The men turned away and went toward Sodom, but Abraham remained standing before the LORD. Then Abraham

approached him and said: "Will you sweep away the righteous with the wicked? What if there are fifty righteous people in the city? Will you really sweep it away and not spare the place for the sake of the fifty righteous people in it? Far be it from you to do such a thing—to kill the righteous with the wicked, treating the righteous and the wicked alike. Far be it from you! Will not the Judge of all the earth do right?"

The LORD said, "If I find fifty righteous people in the city of Sodom, I will spare the whole place for their sake."

Then Abraham spoke up again: "Now that I have been so bold as to speak to the Lord, though I am nothing but dust and ashes, what if the number of the righteous is five less than fifty? Will you destroy the whole city for lack of five people?"

"If I find forty-five there," he said, "I will not destroy it."

Once again he spoke to him, "What if only forty are found there?"

He said, "For the sake of forty, I will not do it."

Then he said, "May the Lord not be angry, but let me speak. What if only thirty can be found there?"

He answered, "I will not do it if I find thirty there."

Abraham said, "Now that I have been so bold as to speak to the Lord, what if only twenty can be found there?"

He said, "For the sake of twenty, I will not destroy it."

Then he said, "May the Lord not be angry, but let me speak just once more. What if only ten can be found there?"

He answered, "For the sake of ten, I will not destroy it."

When the LORD had finished speaking with Abraham, he left, and Abraham returned home. (vv. 22–33)

Abraham is deeply concerned for his nephew Lot, who is lost in the "sin city" of Sodom. When Abraham hears of God's plan to judge and destroy Sodom, his first thought is to intercede on behalf of his unsaved family members, beginning with Lot.

## Negotiating with God

When was the last time you actually took hold of God's promises? Not merely for a day or a week but for months or years. When was the last time you clung to His promises for dear life and wouldn't let go?

You might say, "Well, I prayed for a while. Maybe I didn't pray according to God's will. Maybe that's why my prayer wasn't answered." Perhaps. But then again, maybe you gave up too soon. I'm going to put my neck way out and say that if you are praying God's promises according to God's Word, He *will* answer that prayer.

That's one reason it's a good idea to pray over an open Bible. Take one of God's promises and pray it back to God. Make sure you are not twisting a verse out of context. Make sure you are praying a genuine promise of God and not merely your own wishes projected onto the Scriptures. If you are authentically claiming one of God's promises, which He has given to us in His Word, I believe He will answer your prayer.

For example, 1 Corinthians 7:14 says that an unbelieving spouse is "sanctified" by a believing spouse and that children are "sanctified" by believing parents. *Sanctified* doesn't mean saved. Your faith in Christ can't save your spouse or your children. *Sanctified* means set apart. Your faith in Christ opens a door into your family through which God can work. As you witness to your unsaved family members and pray for them, God works in their lives in powerful ways. They must still come individually to Christ by grace through faith,

154

but your prayers help to open their hearts to receive God's blessing.

If you want to know the level of your spiritual maturity, consider how much time you spend in prayer on behalf of a lost family member, a lost neighbor, or a lost classmate or professor. Are you contending in prayer for God to intervene in their hearts?

Think about the negotiation between God and Abraham regarding the city of Sodom. "Will you sweep away the righteous with the wicked?" asks Abraham. "What if there are fifty righteous people in the city?"

God says, "If I find fifty righteous people in the city of Sodom, I will spare the whole place for their sake."

Abraham continues. What about forty-five people? Forty? Thirty? Twenty? Then he asks, "What if only ten can be found there?"

And God says, "For the sake of ten, I will not destroy it."

This may sound like an auction, but that's the Middle Eastern culture for you. That's just the way things are done over there, even today. You bargain and negotiate for everything. That's what Abraham was doing.

God agreed that even if there were ten righteous people in Sodom, He would spare the city. I suppose Abraham was desperately hoping that there were ten godly people in the city. He dared not try to negotiate any further.

Alas, there were not even ten righteous people in Sodom. But because of his friendship with God, Abraham could boldly ask God to spare his nephew Lot and his family, and God answered that prayer. Abraham had a friend in high places, and so do you. The obedience of faith makes God your friend.

We easily forget that God knows us by name, calls us by name, loves us by name, and cares for us by name. We get into trouble when we forget God's friendship with us and the depth of His love for us. We stop relying on Him and His love for us when we forget that He cares for us in a deeply individual and personal sense. He truly loves us *by name*.

If you are not experiencing friendship with God right now, it's not because of any reluctance on God's part. He wants to have fellowship with you. The problem is that you have allowed sin or some person or some habit or some attitude to come between you and God. No matter where you've been, what you've done, or how you've failed Him, you can be a friend of God today.

He wants to be your friend. Do you want to be His?

## The Birth Pains of History

Are there parallels between Sodom in Abraham's day and America in the twenty-first century? Do you think God looks at our society and says, "The outcry against that civilization is so great and their sin so grievous that I will go down and see"? If God were to search our society, including our churches and our homes, what would He find? And how would He respond?

There are three things the Lord always does before He withdraws His hand of blessing from a nation.

First, He holds an inquest. He inquires into the fact of the matter, to see if the sin of the people is as bad as it appears. He looks at the moral condition of the people and their leaders, including their spiritual leaders.

Second, He makes Himself available. You can pray to Him at any time and any place, and you can repent and seek His forgiveness. You can intercede for others with God. He is accessible. Isaiah 55:6 says, "Seek the LORD while he may be found; call on him while he is near."

Third, no matter how few in number, the righteous will always make a difference. "You are the salt of the earth," the Lord says in the Sermon on the Mount. "You are the light of the world."[3] Salt is a preservative. Light illuminates.

Like salt, we preserve our society against both moral decay and the sudden destruction of God's judgment. But we can only preserve society as long as we are a savor of Christ in our world. If we lose our savor, if we no longer represent Christ to the world, then it won't be long before judgment falls.

We are to be light as well. Light makes reality and truth visible. Light shines on us, highlighting our flaws and deformities, our sins and failures.

How many Christians does it take to be salt and light, preserving and illuminating our culture, our nation, and our neighborhoods with the penetrating power of God's truth? Not many. Don't fall for the notion that we must be great in number in order for God to use us. Ten godly people could have saved Sodom. Jesus said, "For where two or three gather in my name, there am I with them" (Matt. 18:20). It doesn't take many Christians to be salt and light in our society—but it does take you and me.

Every day, we are watching with our own eyes what Jesus called "the beginning of birth pains"[4] of history. We are seeing the rise of false teachers, false messiahs, and demonic doctrines, deceiving many. We hear of wars and rumors of wars, nation rising up against nation, and kingdom against kingdom. We see famines and earthquakes and other natural disasters. We see church leaders turning away from the faith. We see an increase of wickedness, the rise of division and hatred, and the love of many people growing cold. "All these," Jesus said, "are the beginning of birth pains." They are just the beginning. Conditions in the world and in our nation will grow worse. The labor pains are already coming at shorter and shorter intervals and with greater intensity. Are we paralyzed with fear—or are we ready to face the future? Jesus told us what to do when we see these signs: "When these things begin to take place, stand up and lift up your heads, because your redemption is drawing near" (Luke 21:28).

As we look at the sin and violence that have shaken the foundation of our nation, do we despair—or do we lift up our heads? Do we pray, witness, and love as many people into the kingdom of God as we can—or are we, like Lot, lost in "sin city," accommodating to it and partaking in it?

Are we salt? Are we light?

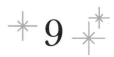

# The Birth of Laughter

In 1964, journalist Norman Cousins was diagnosed with a crippling autoimmune disease, and his doctor told him he had a one in five hundred chance of recovery. Known as one of the world's leading optimists, Cousins refused to accept those dismal odds. He had long believed that our emotions have a great impact on our health and our ability to fight illness. Now he'd have a chance to test his theory.

Working closely with his doctors, he did everything they told him to do in terms of diet and medicine. In addition to his medical treatments, he began treating his disease with laughter. This was long before video streaming or DVDs or even VHS tapes, so Norman Cousins bought a 16mm movie projector and began watching all the comedy films he could find at the library. His favorites were reruns of the *Candid Camera* TV show and old Marx Brothers movies. Those films induced what he called "belly laughter."

Cousins later wrote that he made an amazing discovery: "Ten minutes of solid belly laughter would give me two hours of pain-free sleep. Since my illness involved severe inflammation of the spine and joints, making it painful even to turn over in bed, the practical value of laughter became a significant feature of treatment."[1]

Though not a doctor or formally trained researcher, Cousins published his personal findings about laughter and healing in the *New England Journal of Medicine*, as well as in a bestselling book, *Anatomy of an Illness as Perceived by the Patient*. Norman Cousins was a pioneer in the study of the relationship between laughter and health.

After Cousins opened the door to this field of study, researchers conducted many peer-reviewed studies showing that laughter produces many health benefits, including stimulating the immune system, decreasing harmful stress hormones, increasing pain tolerance, lowering blood pressure, lowering bad cholesterol (LDL), and raising good cholesterol (HDL). Researchers even found that joyous laughter promotes changes in the blood levels of leptin (an energy-balancing hormone) and ghrelin (a hunger-regulating hormone), so that laughter actually mimics the effects of an exercise workout.[2]

God designed these healing functions of the human body, and He told us about them in His Word. Some three thousand years ago, Solomon wrote about the healing wisdom of God in Proverbs 17:22:

> A cheerful heart is good medicine,
>     but a crushed spirit dries up the bones.

Laughter and joy ought to be important parts of the Christian life. The psalmist writes that laughter and joy testify to the world that the Lord is active in our lives, protecting us and giving us victory:

> When the LORD restored the fortunes of Zion,
>     we were like those who dreamed.
> Our mouths were filled with laughter,
>     our tongues with songs of joy.
> Then it was said among the nations,
>     "The LORD has done great things for them."
> The LORD has done great things for us,
>     and we are filled with joy.
>
> Restore our fortunes, LORD,
>     like streams in the Negev.
> Those who sow with tears
>     will reap with songs of joy.
> Those who go out weeping,
>     carrying seed to sow,
> will return with songs of joy,
>     carrying sheaves with them. (Ps. 126)

Those who have the greatest reason to be joyful in all circumstances are those who have placed their trust in the Lord Jesus Christ. Why, then, are we not more joyful? I think part of the reason is that we take ourselves too seriously.

A writer once interviewed me by phone for an article in a leadership magazine for pastors. He said, "Do you have anything to say to young pastors?"

"Yes," I said. "Here's my deeply theological advice for young pastors: take your calling very seriously, but don't take yourself too seriously."

I experience a lot of joy in my ministry as a pastor, and I believe one reason for this joy is that I frequently laugh at myself. Sometimes I'm standing in the pulpit, and I just can't help laughing. The audience looks back at me in bewilderment because I'm the only one laughing. They wonder, *What is he laughing about?* Answer: I'm laughing at myself.

Did you know that God laughs? Four passages in the Old Testament speak of the laughter of God—Psalms 2:4; 37:13; 59:8; and Proverbs 1:26—and God's laughter is always provoked by the folly and arrogance of the wicked. God sees those who would oppose Him, and He thinks they're pretty funny. We have every right to laugh along with God at the folly of the wicked.

## Communicators of Laughter and Joy

In Genesis 21, we come to the story of the birth of laughter. In verses 1–7 of this passage, we see Abraham reach the culmination of year after year of counting stars when he could see none.

> Now the LORD was gracious to Sarah as he had said, and the LORD did for Sarah what he had promised. Sarah became pregnant and bore a son to Abraham in his old age, at the very time God had promised him. Abraham gave the name Isaac to the son Sarah bore him. When his son Isaac was eight days old, Abraham circumcised him, as God commanded him. Abraham was a hundred years old when his son Isaac was born to him.
>
> Sarah said, "God has brought me laughter, and everyone who hears about this will laugh with me." And she added, "Who would have said to Abraham that Sarah would nurse children? Yet I have borne him a son in his old age."

Finally, after all those desolate, desperate years of counting stars while seeing none, Abraham had received his first-ever star. In the desert of the ancient Middle East, you could look up at night and see the stars with startling clarity. God's promise to Abraham was that the number of stars he could see in the night sky would be vastly exceeded by the number of his descendants. Abraham didn't understand it at the time, but God was talking about *spiritual* descendants who would not merely be born through the biological birth process but would be *born again* by grace through faith in Jesus Christ.

I'm sure that whenever Abraham looked up at the heavens on a clear night, he thought of that promise. Perhaps he actually tried to count the stars in the night sky. "One, two, three, four—wait, did I count that one twice? I'd better start over." Even if he counted for decades, he could never be sure of the number.

Finally, when he was a hundred years old and Sarah was ninety, God gave them Star Number One. What did they name him? Isaac. And what does *Isaac* mean in the Hebrew language? Laughter.

The graciousness of our God is astounding. He took Sarah's laughter of unbelief and transformed it into the laughter of joy. He transformed the laughter of incredulousness into the laughter of the indescribable. He transformed the laughter of sarcasm into the laughter of salvation. What a great God we worship! What a mighty God we have!

God brought laughter not only to Sarah. He also brought laughter to generations and generations to come. They would read the story of Sarah and they would laugh.

What was the reason for Abraham's and Sarah's joyful laughter when Isaac was born? I believe the joy they felt at having a baby was secondary to the joy they felt because of their life in the Lord. For the believer, joy comes from living day in and day out with an eternal perspective—God's perspective. That's what distinguishes Christians from secular society. People of this world are focused on this life—on what is happening in the news or to the economy or in government and the political realm.

A 2017 Pew Research Center poll showed that political polarization has become more extreme in the United States than at any other time since the Civil War.[3] I remember a time, decades ago, when a Republican president and a Democratic speaker of the House would get together at the end of the day to socialize, swap stories, and find compromises for the good of the people. Now there is no middle ground between the parties, no compromise, and no civility. People revile and threaten each other on social media. There is no exchanging of views, no listening and learning from one another, just name-calling and hate.

Why? There are many reasons, undoubtedly, but I think one reason for our political polarization today is the decline of faith in America. People used to derive their sense of meaning and significance from their daily walk with God. As people have become more secularized, as the church has declined in influence in America, people no longer have faith to give them a sense of purpose.

As a result, people have replaced the joy of knowing God with the adrenaline rush of attacking and belittling their political foes. They have replaced the joy of knowing God with the pride of thinking themselves morally superior to the other side. As faith in God has declined, so have morality and civility. Anything goes, including the destruction of political opponents, along with their reputations and their families. Scorched-earth, win-at-any-cost politics is the new religion for many Americans.

I believe that Christians should be politically aware and involved, but we must take care not to let politics push Jesus off the throne of our lives. This world is wracked with anger and hatred, and I refuse to be a part of it. If we allow ourselves to get caught up in the name-calling and bare-knuckle tactics of worldly politics, we are no better than the secularists who have declared war on us. The Lord's kingdom is not of this world, and we must never let our political passions take the place of our passion for Christ.

As Christians, we should be people whose lives are characterized by joy and righteous laughter, no matter what is happening in our society. We must pursue justice for the oppressed, food for the hungry, clothing and housing for the needy, the right to life for the unborn, a clean and moral society for our children, and honesty in government. Above all, we must preach the good news of Jesus Christ at every opportunity—but we must not get caught up in the partisan bickering and personal destruction that tear our society apart.

Let our holy, joyous laughter be heard wherever we go. Let us be role models and communicators of joy!

## Joy in Spite of Circumstances

Here we are, four thousand years after the events in Genesis, and we are still drawing encouragement from the story of Abraham and Sarah. After forty centuries, we are still learning from this faithful couple important insights about the faithfulness of God. In spite of their doubts, their partial belief, their failures, and their attempts to take matters into their own hands, God was faithful to His promises and He was faithful to Abraham and Sarah.

They counted stars when they could see none until their first star fell from the sky and into their arms. In the process, Abraham and Sarah learned three all-important life lessons—and so should we.

### Lesson #1: God Always Keeps His Word

Never give up praying for the fulfillment of a promise God has made to you in His Word. Never give up praying for an unsaved family member. Never give up praying for your children—pray as long as your life lasts, even if you don't see the answer in your own lifetime. Never give up praying for God to reveal His will to you. Never give up praying for wisdom and direction in your life. If you are praying the promises of God, He will answer that prayer. God keeps His word all the time.

### Lesson #2: Our God Is a Powerful God

Nothing is too hard for God. He is a mighty God. He is an awesome God. He is the Lord of the impossible. When I talk about the power of God to do what is, humanly speaking, beyond the realm of possibility, someone invariably says to me, "I understand that the Bible says that nothing is too hard for God. I know that God did a miracle for Abraham and Sarah. But you don't know my situation. This is different. My problem is really insoluble. The opposition I face is too great. I'm too old (or too young or too weak or too depressed or too this or too that). God can't solve my problem."

Are we talking about the same God? Isn't your God the same God who opened the womb of a ninety-year-old woman and made her the mother of a boy named Laughter? Isn't your God the same God who enabled a virgin to give birth to the Savior of the world? If Abraham and Sarah had faith in the God of the impossible, why are you serving a god of limitations?

Please understand, when Sarah conceived and went into labor and gave birth to a baby boy, that was just the beginning of the miracle. God also enabled Sarah, at age ninety, to have milk in her breasts to nurse this miraculous child. God enabled Sarah to have the energy to raise this baby, to care for him, and to keep up with him when he became a toddler and went through the "terrible twos."

And the miracle didn't stop even there! Consider Abraham, having a son at a hundred years of age. Moreover, his body was so renewed and rejuvenated by the power of El Shaddai, almighty God, that he fathered six more children after Sarah passed away. When God miraculously heals, it is not a partial healing. God heals all the way. It is a complete restoration.

### Lesson #3: Our God Is Not in Any Hurry to Fulfill His Promises

We are always impatient, always in a rush. But God cannot be stampeded into acting hastily. His wisdom is perfect. His timing is impeccable; His watch is never too fast or too slow. "He has made everything beautiful in its time," writes

Solomon. "He has also set eternity in the human heart; yet no one can fathom what God has done from beginning to end" (Eccles. 3:11).

One of the hardest things we face in the Christian life is what seems to us to be God's delay. Even though His timetable may be years or decades different from ours, God's delay does not mean God's denial. The Word of God is true and the promises of God are dependable.

### Isaac's Birth—A Foreshadowing

Abraham and Sarah were grateful that, after an apparent delay of many years, God gave them a son to complete their joy and fulfill the promise. But Abraham and Sarah could not see the big picture. They didn't know that God had a much larger, grander plan than simply giving Abraham a son and a line of many descendants. Though Abraham's and Sarah's lives were suddenly filled with joy, God had an infinitely greater joy in mind—and Isaac's birth was a link in a chain of circumstances leading to that joy.

The birth of Isaac was the foreshadowing of another supernatural birth that would take place two thousand years after Isaac. The birth of Isaac foreshadowed the birth of Jesus. That's why Jesus said to the hardheaded Pharisees, "Your father Abraham rejoiced at the thought of seeing my day; he saw it and was glad" (John 8:56). The Lord was talking about this very time in Abraham's life, when he saw Jesus prefigured in the life of Isaac.

If you look closely at the life of Isaac, you'll see his life resembles the life of Jesus in many key points. Let me suggest seven similarities between the birth of Isaac and the birth of Jesus.

### Both Births Were Promised by God

In Genesis 3:15, God told the serpent, who was Satan in serpent form:

> And I will put enmity
>> between you and the woman,
>> and between your offspring and hers;
> he will crush your head,
>> and you will strike his heel.

This is a curse to the serpent but a blessing to Adam and Eve. The woman's offspring is Jesus, and though Satan would strike His heel (on the cross), He would crush Satan's head (also on the cross). This was a promise God made in the Garden of Eden that He would send His Son to die on the cross, and through His death and resurrection He would destroy the power of sin and death. That was the first promise of the coming of Jesus, and this promise of God was affirmed again and again throughout Scripture.

### There Was a Long Delay between the Promise and the Fulfillment of the Promise

From the time God first spoke to Abraham in Ur of the Chaldeans until the time Isaac was born was a period of about thirty years. From the time the promise of a Savior was made in the Garden of Eden until Jesus was born in Bethlehem was a period of several thousand years. In both cases, God seemed to delay—and in both cases, God's timing was just right.

### *The Question of Each Mother-to-Be Was Answered in the Same Way*

In Genesis 18:13–14, Sarah asked, "Will I really have a child, now that I am old?" and the Lord answered, "Is anything too hard for the LORD?" In Luke 1:34–37, the angel told Mary she was going to give birth to the baby Jesus. Mary asked, "How will this be since I am a virgin?" The angel replied, "No word from God will ever fail," which is another way of stating that nothing is too hard for the Lord. The answer to the ninety-year-old woman's question was the same as the answer to the young virgin's question: nothing is too hard for the Lord.

### *The Names of Both Isaac and Jesus Were Symbolic*

Both names were given by God Himself. Before Isaac was conceived, God told Abraham to call him Isaac. In Matthew 1:21, God told Joseph in a dream that Mary would give birth to a son—"and you are to give him the name Jesus, because he will save his people from their sins."

### *Both Births Took Place at the Appointed Time*

This is probably the most stunning similarity of all. Like the birth of Isaac, the birth of Jesus took place exactly on God's schedule. Not too early, not too late.

### *Both Births Were Miraculous*

The birth of Jesus is more miraculous than the birth of Isaac, because Jesus was born to a virgin, and His birth involved God becoming a human being. The birth of Isaac was the shadow; the birth of Jesus was the reality. The shadow is not greater than the reality. Isaac was a picture pointing us to a greater reality to come—Jesus the Messiah.

### Both Births Were Occasions of Great Joy

The birth of a child normally brings joy to a family—but the joy that accompanied the birth of Isaac went far beyond the norm. His birth marked the long-awaited fulfillment of God's prophetic promise of a son. At last, Abraham could count a star that he could see and cradle in his arms. The joy of Abraham and Sarah extended far beyond the moment of Isaac's birth and continued from generation to generation.

Mary's unspeakable joy also went far beyond the joy that is normally felt when a baby comes into the world. She was going to give birth to the Savior of the world. Her joy is also your joy and mine. It's the joy of millions of people who have looked to that baby with eyes of faith and have found salvation through faith in the Lord Jesus Christ. That is why Mary sings the Magnificat, her song of joy—not only her own individual joy but the joy of salvation that she shares with all who will place their trust in the Son.

> My soul glorifies the Lord
> and my spirit rejoices in God my Savior,
> for he has been mindful
> of the humble state of his servant.
> From now on all generations will call me blessed,
> for the Mighty One has done great things for
> me—
> holy is his name.

His mercy extends to those who fear him,
  from generation to generation.
He has performed mighty deeds with his arm;
  he has scattered those who are proud in their in-
    most thoughts.
He has brought down rulers from their thrones
  but has lifted up the humble.
He has filled the hungry with good things
  but has sent the rich away empty.
He has helped his servant Israel,
  remembering to be merciful
to Abraham and his descendants forever,
  just as he promised our ancestors. (Luke 1:46–55)

The joy of Mary and Joseph had nothing to do with the surrounding circumstances. Based on their circumstances, they should have been miserable, not joyful. They were poor, lodging in a filthy stable, their baby laid in a donkey's feed trough in place of a cradle. They were betrothed but not yet wed, so Mary was an outcast, viewed by her community as a girl who had behaved immorally. This was an offense that could have gotten her stoned to death in that society. Yet Mary felt *joy*! Her soul exalted the Lord.

The salvation you and I have received was made possible by that little bundle of joy in the manger of the stable. We are saved because that baby was born to a virgin. And because of that baby, you and I can have *joy* regardless of our circumstances. We can have *peace* regardless of our surroundings. We can have *contentment* regardless of the events in our lives.

So the question is—do you have joy, or have you lost your joy?

172

## Isaac's Birth and Spiritual Rebirth

Every human being ever born of a woman needs to experience not just *one* birth but *two* births. The second birth is a rebirth, and Jesus called it being "born again." Just as there are similarities between the birth of Isaac and the birth of the Lord Jesus Christ, I believe there are three similarities between Isaac's birth and our spiritual rebirth.

### The Birth of Isaac and Spiritual Rebirth Are Humanly Impossible

The bodies of Abraham and Sarah, for all intents and purposes, were dead. Though they were living, the reproductive systems of their bodies were dead. And here's an amazing analogy. Before our hearts were regenerated and the Holy Spirit awakened us to our desperate need for salvation, we too were living yet dead. We were biologically alive but spiritually dead. We were not asleep or in a coma; we were dead in our sins. We could do nothing to save ourselves. It took a miraculous and supernatural intervention of God to raise us from our spiritual death. We could no more raise ourselves to new spiritual life than a ninety-year-old woman could give birth to a new human life.

Unless you are born again, you will not see heaven. That's the bottom line. You could go to church all your life and even go to seminary and become a preacher. But if you are not born again, you will not go to heaven. And believe me, there are many preachers in pulpits across America and around the world who have never been born again. Church attendance does not save you. Only the second birth saves you. If you have received Jesus as your Lord and Savior, and you have been born again by the Spirit of God, you have had a supernatural birth.

### The Miraculous Birth of Isaac and the Supernatural Spiritual Birth Both Take Place by Faith

The Bible tells us that Abraham "believed the LORD, and he credited it to him as righteousness" (Gen. 15:6). What did Abraham believe? He believed in who God is, and he believed in the promises God had made to him, including the promise that he would have more descendants than the stars in the sky.

That's faith! You and I are raised spiritually to life because we have placed our trust and faith in Jesus as our Lord and Savior—and God credits our faith to us as righteousness. That is why we have been spiritually reborn.

### Isaac Was Born and We Have Been Reborn So That God Would Receive the Glory

In his Letter to the Romans, Paul writes:

> Against all hope, Abraham in hope believed and so became the father of many nations, just as it had been said to him, "So shall your offspring be." Without weakening in his faith, he faced the fact that his body was as good as dead—since he was about a hundred years old—and that Sarah's womb was also dead. Yet he did not waver through unbelief regarding the promise of God, but was strengthened in his faith *and gave glory to God*, being fully persuaded that God had power to do what he had promised. (Rom. 4:18–21, emphasis added)

Isaac's birth resulted in greater glory for God. Our second birth results in greater glory for God. We can't be saved by our own good works. If we could save ourselves with good works, then we would get the glory, not God. It is God who has done all the work—whether it is the work of opening Sarah's womb or the work of saving us through the death of Jesus on the cross. As Paul says, "For it is by grace you have been saved, through faith—and this is not from yourselves, it is the gift of God—not by works, so that no one can boast" (Eph. 2:8–9).

## Salvation, Joy, and Laughter

The story of Abraham in Genesis, like the gospel story, was written so that we might believe. The story of Abraham tells us that it was Abraham's faith that was credited to him as righteousness. The gospel story, the story of Jesus the Messiah, tells us that it is faith that saves us as well: "For God so loved the world that he gave his one and only Son, that *whoever believes in him* shall not perish but have eternal life" (John 3:16, emphasis added).

God is saying to us through these stories: "I put the Bible in your hands for a reason: I want you to be born again. I want you to be safe with Me in heaven for eternity. I want you to put your trust in Me, live for Me, serve Me, and spread My good news to everyone around. I want you to be like Abraham—I want you to be My friend."

What a great God is our God. He is El Shaddai, the mighty God. He is the God who always keeps His promises. He is the faithful God, the God who deserves all the praise and all the glory. He is the God who called Abraham "friend," and He is the God who seeks friendship with you and me.

He brings us *salvation*. He brings us *joy*. And praise be to God, He brings us *laughter*.

# 10

# Abraham's Stars

In 2004, a book launched a cultural phenomenon. That book was *The End of Faith* by neuroscientist Sam Harris. The cultural phenomenon was called "the New Atheism."

The old atheism was content to merely mock and criticize religion while coexisting with religious people. Atheists considered Christians and other religious people to be foolish and superstitious but essentially harmless. But the old atheism came to an end after the terrorist attacks in New York City and Washington, DC, on September 11, 2001.

As a result of those deadly attacks, Sam Harris and his fellow New Atheists (including biologist Richard Dawkins and journalist Christopher Hitchens) became convinced that religion—*all* religion, not just militant Islam—poses a threat to the existence of the human race. Though it was Muslim extremists who carried out the 9/11 attacks, not Baptists or Episcopalians, the New Atheists seemed to direct most of their ire at Christians. In fact, Harris's follow-up to *The End of Faith* was a 2006 book called *Letter to a Christian Nation*, which he wrote "to demolish the intellectual and moral pretensions of Christianity in its most committed forms."[1]

The logic of the New Atheists' hatred for Christianity is hard to follow. Christians do not fly airplanes into buildings on orders from God. In the Sermon on the Mount, Jesus tells us, "Blessed are the peacemakers, for they will be called children of God" and "Love your enemies and pray for those who persecute you, that you may be children of your Father in heaven."[2] So how are Christians a threat to human existence?

If Sam Harris wanted to prevent future 9/11s, it seems logical that he would have written a book called *Letter to the Muslim Nation*. It is the Qur'an, after all, not the Bible, that says, "I will cast terror into the hearts of those who disbelieve. Therefore strike off their heads and strike off every fingertip of them"[3] and "Fight those who do not believe in Allah."[4]

Though the New Atheists condemn Islamic terrorism, they condemn Christianity and Judaism just as harshly, if not more so. One New Atheist even advocates the totalitarian notion that the state should forbid Christian parents to teach their faith to their children—and parents who violate that law should lose custody of their children.[5] An ideology that would deny First Amendment religious liberty is not just a "New" Atheism but deserves to be called Militant Radical Atheism.

One biblical account militant atheists love to mock is the story we now come to—the account of God's command that Abraham sacrifice his son Isaac. Christopher Hitchens, who passed away in 2011, critiqued the story of Abraham and

178

Isaac in his 2007 bestseller *god Is Not Great* (his use of the
lowercase god instead of God is deliberate).

> Abraham agreed to murder his son. He prepared the kin-
> dling, laid the tied-up boy upon it . . . and took up the knife
> in order to kill the child like an animal. At the last available
> moment his hand was stayed, not by god as it happens, but
> by an angel, and he was praised from the clouds for showing
> his sturdy willingness to murder an innocent in expiation of
> his own crimes. As a reward for his fealty, he was promised
> a long and large posterity.[6]

And Richard Dawkins, in his book *The God Delusion*,
calls this incident in Abraham's life "the infamous tale of
the sacrificing of his son Isaac."[7] He recaps the story in his
own words:

> God ordered Abraham to make a burnt offering of his longed-
> for son. Abraham built an altar, put firewood upon it, and
> trussed Isaac up on top of the wood. His murdering knife was
> already in his hand when an angel dramatically intervened with
> the news of a last-minute change of plan: God was only joking
> after all, "tempting" Abraham, and testing his faith. A modern
> moralist cannot help but wonder how a child could ever recover
> from such psychological trauma. By the standards of modern
> morality, this disgraceful story is an example simultaneously
> of child abuse, bullying in two asymmetrical power relation-
> ships, and the first recorded use of the Nuremberg defense: "I
> was only obeying orders." Yet the legend is one of the great
> foundational myths of all three monotheistic religions. . . .
>   Apologists even seek to salvage some decency for the God
> character in this deplorable tale. Wasn't it good of God to
> spare Isaac's life at the last minute?[8]

These New Atheist writers don't quote the biblical account but prefer to retell it in a distorted form. In the process, they have missed the meaning and majesty of this story—and that is why they fail to understand why it has endured for thousands of years as an example of faith in the living God.

## A PhD from the University of Faith

When my children were growing up, they hated watching television with me, because after watching a show for ten minutes, I'd know the ending. I'd say, "That guy will turn out to be the criminal" or "Those two will end up at the altar." TV scripts tend to follow a predictable format, because TV writers know that viewers like a certain kind of ending.

But reality is never so easy to predict—especially when God is involved in the story. The Genesis account of the life of Abraham has the ring of truth despite the miraculous nature of the events. If you were going to turn this story into a TV show, the logical place to end the story would be Genesis 21, the birth of Isaac. The story line would be this: Abraham is called by God, he obeys then fails, obeys then fails, until Isaac, the son of promise, is born. The music swells, fadeout. The End.

Abraham's story, however, doesn't end that way. It takes an unexpected turn. After years of waiting on God's promise, the son is born. Then, incredibly, God tells Abraham to take his son up on a mountain and sacrifice him.

Now, that's a plot twist! You can never leave surprises out of the equation when the story comes from God's Word. Here's how the story begins:

Some time later God tested Abraham. He said to him, "Abraham!"

"Here I am," he replied.

Then God said, "Take your son, your only son, whom you love—Isaac—and go to the region of Moriah. Sacrifice him there as a burnt offering on a mountain I will show you."

Early the next morning Abraham got up and loaded his donkey. He took with him two of his servants and his son Isaac. When he had cut enough wood for the burnt offering, he set out for the place God had told him about. On the third day Abraham looked up and saw the place in the distance. He said to his servants, "Stay here with the donkey while I and the boy go over there. We will worship and then we will come back to you." (Gen. 22:1–5)

God spoke and told Abraham to take Isaac, the son of promise, and sacrifice him as a burnt offering. The mind recoils from God's command. We think, *This is murder.* Nowhere else in the Bible does God ever demand a human sacrifice. (Opponents of the Bible cite Jephthah in Judges 12 as an example of human sacrifice in the Bible, but God didn't command Jephthah to commit such an act. It was the result of Jephthah's foolish vow, and it's not clear that he carried it out.)

From a human point of view, this is one of the most perplexing incidents in all of Scripture. I confess to you I cannot fully fathom it. Taking this story at face value, without attempting to understand its deeper meaning, it's easy to see why New Atheist writers would single it out for criticism. I don't deny the difficulties posed by this account, but there is a bigger picture to this story that opponents of the Bible completely miss.

This event must be understood in the context of Abraham's entire life, including the many times Abraham's faith had faltered and failed. Without understanding Abraham's life, it becomes easy to say that this is a story about a cruel God who played a malevolent prank on Abraham and Isaac. But the point of this story is to illustrate how far Abraham has come in his faith.

God first called Abraham out of Ur of the Chaldeans some fifty years earlier. Those fifty years were Abraham's school of faith. It's a school we all go through in the Christian life. Abraham entered the school of faith when he lived in Ur and God spoke to him and promised to make of him a great nation.

When Abraham answered God's call and set off for Canaan, he entered his kindergarten years in the school of faith. He fumbled his way through those early years, demonstrating faith and obedience when he built an altar at Bethel and failing miserably when he drifted into Egypt and lied to Pharaoh. When God led him out of Egypt and back into the land of promise, Abraham graduated from kindergarten in the school of faith.

Later, after Abraham rescued Lot and gave one tenth of his net worth to Melchizedek, King of Salem, he graduated from the elementary grades in the school of faith. He still had much to learn and far to go. He got held back a year when he tried to force God's timetable by fathering Ishmael with Sarah's maid. Years later, when Ishmael was a teenager and Abraham was in his high school years in the school of faith, Abraham called out to God, "Let Ishmael be the son of promise! Ishmael will do. I'm happy to settle for second best." But God said no.

Abraham finally graduated with a bachelor's degree from the University of Faith when he trusted God to give him a son by Sarah. When that son was born, Abraham and Sarah named him Isaac.

Even though Abraham has his bachelor's degree, his education is not complete. Faith is like a muscle, and it only grows when you exercise it. God has been putting Abraham through a program of spiritual calisthenics for about five decades. Now it's time for the ultimate test of the strength of Abraham's faith. Now his faith will be challenged at an entirely new level. Abraham has never confronted any challenge to his faith like this one.

In Genesis 22, we see Abraham in the PhD program of God's University of Faith. A doctorate is the highest degree you can earn, and Abraham is earning his PhD in trusting God. In a PhD program, you take five examinations after three or four years of coursework. Each examination is five hours long. They are called "comprehensives" for a reason. As part of a PhD program, the doctoral candidate also writes a dissertation. It must be original work, not simply regurgitated from secondary sources. The doctoral degree program is rigorous because this is the pinnacle of the educational system.

When Abraham takes his son Isaac up that mountain, he is completing the final requirements for his PhD program. When he returns from the mountain, he will be Dr. Abraham.

## How This Story Speaks to Us

God called Abraham and told him, "Take your son, your only son, whom you love—Isaac—and go to the region of

Moriah. Sacrifice him there as a burnt offering on a mountain I will show you." After all these years of walking with the Lord, Abraham knows God's voice. He's used to hearing this voice. But this time, the voice of God shatters his peaceful existence. God's command is like a dagger in Abraham's heart. The command God gives Abraham is devastating. How could God ask this of the man He calls His friend?

Notice how clear, definite, and specific God is: "Take your son, your only son, whom you love—Isaac." God wants there to be no mistake. He is speaking of the very son God gave Abraham in fulfillment of His promise. God was not asking for Ishmael to be sacrificed but Isaac, the boy named Laughter. To make doubly sure there is no mistaking God's meaning, He adds "your only son, whom you love."

Where are they going? To a mountain in the region of Moriah. According to 2 Chronicles 3:1, the Temple Mount in Jerusalem was known as Mount Moriah and is one of the mountains of the Moriah region. Some scholars suggest that the place where God told Abraham to sacrifice Isaac may have been the hill later known as Calvary where Jesus was crucified.

It is easy to imagine what Abraham might have said when God told him to sacrifice Isaac: "Couldn't I offer a hundred rams or a hundred head of cattle instead, Lord? Couldn't I offer myself? I've lived long enough—put me on the altar and slay me, Lord! Remember all the miraculous works You have done, Lord? Remember how my friends and neighbors gave glory to You because of Your amazing works? If You ask this of me, Your reputation will be destroyed, Your testimony will be ruined!"

Here's what amazes me about this story: Abraham never said any of those things. If he had, I'm sure it would have been recorded in Genesis 22. But Abraham didn't object. He didn't beg. He didn't argue. Instead, he obeyed. The text tells us that, early the next morning, Abraham got up and prepared to make the trip to the mountains of Moriah.

The Bible tells us that God's command to Abraham was a test. God had richly blessed Abraham and Sarah with a long-promised, long-anticipated son, Isaac. Sometimes God's gifts and blessings become so dear to us that they begin to take God's place in our lives. Perhaps God wanted to make Abraham aware that Isaac was taking God's place in his life. God already knew the state of Abraham's heart, the depth of his faith, the state of Abraham's friendship with God. This test wasn't intended to tell God anything He didn't already know. It was intended to demonstrate an important truth to Abraham himself. He was going to find out how much he really trusted God. He was going to find out just how strong his faith in God really was.

At the same time, God is speaking to you and me through the example of Abraham. Let me ask you this: Have any of God's gifts begun to take God's place in your life? Have any of God's blessings begun to replace Him in your thoughts, your time, and your affections? Those blessings might be material things or ways you spend your time or even people in your life. Would you be willing to "sacrifice" those gifts, let go of them, in order to make God the number one priority in your life once more?

## Abraham's Logical Decision

Please don't miss the main issue of this story. God has made it clear that salvation is going to come through Isaac. For

185

the first time, Abraham is now confronted with a conflict—a huge conflict between the promises of God and the command of God. How will he resolve it? He can conclude that God is a liar who goes back on His promises. Or he can conclude that God is erratic, capricious, and doesn't know His own mind. Either conclusion would be devastating.

But wait—there is another possibility: Abraham can simply trust without questioning. A god who lies and goes back on His promises is not the God he has grown to know and love. And the God who calls him friend has never been erratic or capricious in the past. El Shaddai has always kept His word and has always been steady, dependable, and trustworthy.

In the face of God's seemingly impossible command, Abraham makes a decision to trust God. Even if it means the death of Isaac and the revoking of all of God's promises to Abraham? Yes, Abraham would continue to trust God—no matter what.

We don't know what went through Abraham's mind when God gave him this command. The Bible doesn't tell us. There are a few clues and hints but no definitive statement of Abraham's thoughts. We find one important insight into Abraham's thinking in the New Testament Letter to the Hebrews:

> By faith Abraham, when God tested him, offered Isaac as a sacrifice. He who had embraced the promises was about to sacrifice his one and only son, even though God had said to him, "It is through Isaac that your offspring will be reckoned." Abraham reasoned that God could even raise the dead, and so in a manner of speaking he did receive Isaac back from death. (Heb. 11:17–19)

Abraham believed that God would resurrect Isaac. Why did he believe that? No one had ever come back from the dead before. There was no reason for Abraham to suppose that God would raise Isaac from the dead.

I believe Abraham concluded that God would raise Isaac for the simple reason that he trusted in God's promises. God had promised to give Abraham descendants more numerous than the stars in the sky and that those descendants would come through Isaac. The son of promise could not have descendants if he was dead. Abraham, whose faith had failed in the past, had reached a place where his faith in God's promises was absolute and unconditional. He trusted those promises so completely that when God told him to slay his son Isaac, Abraham did not hesitate. Abraham knew the voice of God and trusted God implicitly.

A skeptic might ask, "How did the writer of Hebrews know what was in the mind of Abraham? Hebrews was written two thousand years after Abraham died." That's true, but skeptics of the Bible look at it from a purely human level. Skeptics think of the Bible as a book composed by more than forty human writers. Believers view the Bible as a book with forty-plus writers but only one author. (A friend of mine said that when the human writers were writing the Bible, the Holy Spirit jumped into the ink!) The Holy Spirit is the author of the Bible. The same Spirit who inspired and directed the writing of Genesis also inspired and directed the writing of Hebrews centuries later.

The writer of Hebrews said Abraham embraced God's promises, and in view of those promises, "*Abraham reasoned that God could even raise the dead.*" Notice the words I emphasized: Abraham reasoned. Based on his past experience with God and his absolute faith in God's promises, *Abraham reached a reasonable, logical conclusion*—supported by a lifetime of evidence—that he was going to receive Isaac back from the dead.

No one had ever been raised from the dead before—but then, no woman had ever had a baby at age ninety before. Is anything too hard for the Lord? No! When you look at the full context of Abraham's entire life, his decision to obey God's command to sacrifice Isaac no longer seems as insane as the New Atheists would have us believe. In fact, given the strength of Abraham's faith and the uniqueness of his long, close friendship with God, his decision to obey was a reasoned and logical decision.

## Where Is the Lamb?

Now, with the benefit of hindsight, we know that the command God gave to Abraham was merely a test. God had no intention of allowing Abraham to kill his son Isaac—but Abraham didn't know that. And because Abraham passed this test, God allowed Abraham to see something nobody else had ever seen before. Abraham was permitted to see, in compelling symbolic terms, how God planned to save the entire human race.

God was going to do the very thing He spared Abraham from doing. God was going to sacrifice His only Son. He was going to send His Son to earth to die in our place, on our behalf, for our sins. That was God's intention all along. He intended that the story of Abraham's near-sacrifice of Isaac would point all of Isaac's descendants to a future day when Jesus, the Lamb of God, would die for all of humanity.

Some two thousand years later, on a mountain in the Moriah range, God offered His one and only Son as a sacrifice for our salvation.

One heartbreaking moment in this story underscores the symbolic connection between the sacrifice of Isaac and the sacrifice of Jesus the Messiah:

> Abraham took the wood for the burnt offering and placed it on his son Isaac, and he himself carried the fire and the knife. As the two of them went on together, Isaac spoke up and said to his father Abraham, "Father?"
>
> "Yes, my son?" Abraham replied.
>
> "The fire and wood are here," Isaac said, "but where is the lamb for the burnt offering?"
>
> Abraham answered, "God himself will provide the lamb for the burnt offering, my son." And the two of them went on together. (Gen. 22:6–8)

Note that Abraham handed the wood to Isaac. So Isaac carried the wood himself to the place where he was to be sacrificed—just as Jesus would later carry the wooden cross on which He was crucified.

Isaac said, "Where is the lamb for the burnt offering?" Isaac's question will be answered by the death of Jesus the Messiah, the Lamb of God, on the cross of Calvary. All the Old Testament animal sacrifices pointed to the perfect sinless Lamb of God who was slain on the cross. Abraham's answer to Isaac's question was a word of prophecy about the coming of Jesus. Abraham said, "God himself will provide the lamb for the burnt offering."

The question Isaac asked—"Where is the lamb?"—would echo through the ages as one Old Testament writer after another wrote about the coming of the Messiah. Isaiah wrote:

> He was oppressed and afflicted,
> yet he did not open his mouth;
> he was led like a lamb to the slaughter,
> and as a sheep before its shearers is silent,
> so he did not open his mouth. (Isa. 53:7)

Century after century, the question "Where is the lamb?" went unanswered until a man from Galilee arrived at the Jordan River, calling people to repentance and baptizing them. As Jesus of Nazareth approached, John said to all the people around him, "Look, the Lamb of God, who takes away the sin of the world!" (John 1:29).

Then John told the people what he had witnessed:

> I saw the Spirit come down from heaven as a dove and remain on him. And I myself did not know him, but the one who sent me to baptize with water told me, "The man on whom you see the Spirit come down and remain is the one who will baptize with the Holy Spirit." I have seen and I testify that this is God's Chosen One. (vv. 32–34)

This is the answer to Isaac's question. It is *this* Lamb of God—Jesus—whom Abraham believed in. It is *this* Lamb of God—Jesus—to whom every faithful Old Testament believer looked forward. It is *this* Lamb of God—Jesus—who is our Shepherd. It is *this* Lamb of God—Jesus—who alone can wash away our sin and guilt and shame by His blood shed upon the cross. And it is *this* Lamb of God—Jesus— who will come again, and He may come at any moment, even as you are reading these words, to judge the living and the dead.

## A Story of Love

This story in Genesis 22 reaches its crisis at verse 9 as Abraham proceeds to carry out the unthinkable command of the Lord:

> When they reached the place God had told him about, Abraham built an altar there and arranged the wood on it. He bound his son Isaac and laid him on the altar, on top of the wood. Then he reached out his hand and took the knife to slay his son. But the angel of the LORD called out to him from heaven, "Abraham! Abraham!"
>
> "Here I am," he replied.
>
> "Do not lay a hand on the boy," he said. "Do not do anything to him. Now I know that you fear God, because you have not withheld from me your son, your only son."
>
> Abraham looked up and there in a thicket he saw a ram caught by its horns. He went over and took the ram and sacrificed it as a burnt offering instead of his son. So Abraham called that place The LORD Will Provide. And to this day it is said, "On the mountain of the LORD it will be provided." (vv. 9–14)

Abraham named the place Yahweh Jireh—the Lord will provide. That name is the same in the three great languages of the ancient Middle East: Hebrew, Aramaic, and Arabic. Abraham was literally saying that God Himself would provide a Savior. God Himself would provide a way out of this dilemma between His mercy and His justice. God Himself

191

would provide a solution to humanity's predicament. Whatever hard times and tough issues you might be facing right now, God will provide a way out. He will provide healing. He will provide vindication. He will provide salvation.

How can we describe the love of God? How can we understand it? How can we measure the depths of it? The story of Abraham and Isaac was given to us to help us understand God's love for us. We look at the act that Abraham is about to commit—the slaying of his own son, the son of promise, his beloved Isaac—and we say, "How can a father do that to his only son?"

And then the realization hits us: that is what the Father did to His only Son. The Lord wants us to understand what it cost Him to send Jesus to be our Savior. He wants us to understand what it means to sacrifice your only Son on the altar so that others might live forever. If you've never before looked at the sacrifice of Jesus from the perspective of God the Father, look closely at this story in Genesis 22. Put yourself in Abraham's place—and in the place of God the Father. Imagine the dread and horror you would feel, looking into the eyes of your son as you raise the knife over his chest.

Perhaps even an atheist could begin to understand the meaning and importance of this story. It's not a story about child abuse or blind obedience, as the New Atheists have claimed. This is a story about love. For God so loved the world that He gave His only begotten Son—that's the reality. The story of Abraham and Isaac on a mountain in Moriah—that's the shadow that points to the reality.

And there's something else about the indomitable faith of Abraham that I don't want you to miss. Abraham says to his servants, "Stay here with the donkey while I and the boy go over there. We will worship and then *we will come back* to you." Abraham told his servants that they were both going to return.

Some people read those words and assume that Abraham was lying to the servants. But Abraham wasn't lying. He would not have lied while carrying out an act of obedience to God. He told the servants exactly what he believed would happen. He had such confidence that God would raise Isaac from the dead that he made this promise to his servants: "We will come back."

## The Faith of Isaac

And let's not forget Isaac's all-important role in this story. Most Bible scholars place Isaac's age at between fifteen and thirty at the time of these events. Isaac was a strong young man, and Abraham was well over a hundred. Isaac could have easily overpowered his father and run away. He could have said, "Father, you're going to do *what*? No way—you're not going to sacrifice me! I'm outta here!" And Abraham could not have stopped him.

I believe that, once Isaac understood what Abraham was about to do, he submitted willingly, out of his own faith in God. He knew the story of his own miraculous birth. He knew about the promises God had made to Abraham. I believe Isaac submitted to death upon that wooden altar the same way Jesus submitted to death upon that wooden cross. So when an atheist wonders how a child could recover from such trauma, I say we need to give Isaac more credit. From the words and example of Abraham, Isaac learned to trust God.

Abraham didn't have to chase Isaac down and tie him up against his will. Isaac wasn't traumatized—he was obedient to God's will, just as Abraham was. I can picture Isaac holding out his hands and saying, "Bind me, Father. Tie my hands and feet. I'm not afraid of death. I'm only afraid that I might flinch, so make sure I can't move, Father. I commend my life to the Lord."

How many times do we claim to love the Lord—but only if it costs us nothing? We love the Lord if the price is right. We love the Lord, but we refuse to surrender anything to Him. We love the Lord, but only if we keep all of His blessings for ourselves. We love the Lord, but only if we don't have to give up the idols in our lives. We love the Lord, but we refuse to give up our wrong relationships, destructive habits, and sinful pleasures.

Isaac knew God had promised that salvation would come through his descendants. He knew he was the miracle child, that son of promise. If you are a parent, you need to be aware that everything you teach your children through your words and your example is engraved on their hearts. It is etched into their lives. If they live to be a hundred, they will never forget what you have taught them.

Abraham and Sarah had etched faith and character into Isaac's heart, day by day by day. Isaac had learned that he could trust his father—and his father's God. He too believed that if he died, God would raise him again.

## Six Traits of Obedience

Abraham's obedience is instructive to us as Christians today. God won't call us to slay our children—that was a unique test of a unique Old Testament saint. But God may call us to do something that seems humanly impossible. He may call us to share Christ with a hostile and unfriendly neighbor. He may call us to attempt to make peace with a longtime enemy. He may call us to volunteer to reach out to needy children in a rough neighborhood. He may call us to befriend an atheist or a Muslim with the goal of witnessing to them about Jesus.

What impossible thing is God calling you to dare for His sake? Are you willing and ready to obey His call? If you want to see what true faith looks like, what true obedience looks like, take a close look at the story of Abraham's willingness to obey God and sacrifice Isaac. As we look at that story, we can identify six traits that characterize the obedience of Abraham.

### Trait #1: Abraham's Obedience Was Prompt

God called, "Abraham!" and he responded instantly, "Here I am, Lord." God gave him his instructions for sacrificing his son, and the next thing we read is "Early the next morning Abraham got up." Not the following week or month but early the next morning. This was the pattern of Abraham's life, once his faith had reached maturity. When God told Abraham to circumcise all the men in his household, Abraham obeyed promptly. When God told Abraham to let Hagar and Ishmael go, Abraham obeyed promptly. So it was only natural that when God said, "Offer your son to Me," Abraham obeyed promptly.

### Trait #2: Abraham's Obedience Was Sustained

Abraham's obedience endured over time. Yes, he went through stages. His faith sometimes faltered or failed. But he responded in faith when God called him out of Ur of the

Chaldeans, and he sustained his faith and increased in faith over the long haul. Finally, some fifty years after God first called him, his faith had grown to the point at which he was willing to obey God, promptly and without argument, when God called Abraham to do the unthinkable.

### Trait #3: Abraham's Obedience Was Willing

Our obedience is often a reluctant obedience. We sense the call of God, and we know we should obey. But we say, "Lord, I'm not sure if that's really Your voice. I'm not sure You really want me to share Christ with that guy. I'm not sure You really want me to tell my Christian friend a hard truth she needs to hear. I'm not sure You are really calling me to maintain godly business ethics when doing so will cost me thousands of dollars." When our obedience is put to the test, we are reluctant to obey.

Abraham demonstrated willing obedience. He did what God commanded without argument or delay. He heard the voice of God, and he acted. We see this same willing obedience in the Garden of Gethsemane when Jesus prayed to the Father the night before He was crucified: "Father, if you are willing, take this cup from me; yet not my will, but yours be done" (Luke 22:42). And Hebrews 10:7 tells us that, when Jesus came into the world, He said to the Father, "Here I am—it is written about me in the scroll—I have come to do your will, my God."

### Trait #4: Abraham's Obedience Was Settled

We say we really, really want to obey God, and we do—for a while. We forsake that sinful habit—until our commitment weakens or the temptation intensifies. We gladly obey God and witness to the people at school or work or in the neighborhood—but then we encounter a grumpy person who is offended by "all this Jesus talk," and fearing another hostile encounter, we stop witnessing and stop obeying the Lord's Great Commission to spread the gospel. We want to obey God with our finances—but we're saving up for a vacation or the budget's a little tight because of the veterinary bill, and the first place we decide to economize is in our offerings to God.

Abraham didn't let changing circumstances affect his obedience. If God said, "Move from this place to that place," Abraham moved. If God said, "Circumcise all the males in your household," he circumcised them. If God said, "Sacrifice your son Isaac," he prepared to sacrifice his son. He didn't say, "I'd like to obey You, Lord, but the circumstances have changed. These conditions are different. You understand why I can't obey You this time." No, Abraham said nothing of the kind. His obedience was settled.

### Trait #5: Abraham's Obedience Was Contagious

Abraham's faith inspired others to believe wholeheartedly and commit everything to God. Think of the millions of believers in Christian history who have read the story of Abraham and his obedience. Though I'm sure no one would want to be tested to the max as Abraham was, many have cried out, "Lord, I want to have the faith of Abraham, a faith that is obedient to You, no matter what. Lord, that's how I want my relationship with You to be." Abraham's faith is inspiring and contagious.

### Trait #6: Abraham's Obedience Was Rewarded

Abraham obeyed, and his obedience was rewarded by God.

> The angel of the LORD called to Abraham from heaven a second time and said, "I swear by myself, declares the LORD, that because you have done this and have not withheld your son, your only son, I will surely bless you and make your descendants as numerous as the stars in the sky and as the sand on the seashore. Your descendants will take possession of the cities of their enemies, and through your offspring all nations on earth will be blessed, because you have obeyed me." (Gen. 22:15–18)

God once again reaffirmed His covenant to Abraham. Obedience is not always rewarded immediately, but it is always rewarded. Abraham was not rewarded instantly, but he was rewarded abundantly. And God did not merely reaffirm His past promise that Abraham's descendants would be more numerous than the stars in the sky. This time, God also gave Abraham an extra promise: He would make Abraham's descendants as numerous "as the sand on the seashore."

Please don't miss this. The Bible makes it clear that God is faithful, but God is also going to reward faithfulness. God will be a debtor to no one. He will not be beholden to you or indebted to you. He will reward your obedience and shower you with blessings. As the apostle Paul reminds us, "God is able to bless you abundantly, so that in all things at all times, having all that you need, you will abound in every good work" (2 Cor. 9:8).

## The Obedience of Jesus

It may surprise you to know that Jesus was rewarded for His obedience on earth. Paul wrote that Jesus "humbled himself by becoming obedient to death—even death on a cross!" Because of His obedience,

> God exalted him to the highest place
>     and gave him the name that is above every name,
> that at the name of Jesus every knee should bow,
>     in heaven and on earth and under the earth,
> and every tongue acknowledge that Jesus Christ is
>     Lord,
>     to the glory of God the Father. (Phil. 2:9–11)

Jesus demonstrated the ultimate form of obedience, and God gave Him the ultimate reward—exaltation and glory at the right hand of God the Father. This reward is the fulfillment of an Old Testament prophecy of the Messiah:

> You make known to me the path of life;
>     you will fill me with joy in your presence,
>     with eternal pleasures at your right hand. (Ps.
>     16:11)

Jesus, the Son of God, exemplified perfect obedience for you and me. He came from the highest place and descended to the lowest place, suffering the agony, humiliation, and loneliness that come from taking our sins onto Himself. Then God the Father "raised Christ from the dead and seated him at his right hand in the heavenly realms, far above all rule and authority, power and dominion, and every name that is invoked, not only in the present age but also in the one to come" (Eph. 1:20–21).

199

One day, maybe sooner than we think, we are going to hear Jesus say, "Well done, good and faithful servant! . . . Come and share your master's happiness!" (Matt. 25:21). And we will receive the reward for our faith and obedience in this life.

For his faith and obedience, Abraham was rewarded with the promise of many descendants, more numerous than the sands of the seashore. His descendants are related to him not by DNA but by faith. His faith pointed ahead to the coming Messiah. Our faith looks back to the death and resurrection of the same Messiah. Abraham's obedient willingness to sacrifice his son Isaac points ahead to the Father's willingness to sacrifice His Son out of love for you and me.

The promise of Abraham's reward is being fulfilled even now. You and I are his reward, his descendants according to faith. When you prayed to receive Jesus as your Lord and Savior, you joined Abraham's family and became one more fulfillment of God's promise to him when he was still in Ur of the Chaldeans.

Through most of his life, Abraham counted stars, even when he could see none. Today, Abraham's stars are everywhere, in every nation, speaking every language, all worshiping the same God he worshiped and praising the same Lord Jesus he looked forward to. Abraham's descendants number in the billions. They are far more numerous than the stars in the sky. And here's a thought that should bring tears of joy to our eyes and send a thrill up our spines: You and I are Abraham's stars.

# Notes

## Chapter 1 Seven Promises

1. Wikipedia, s.v. "Tycho Brahe," accessed March 18, 2019, https://en.wiki pedia.org/wiki/Tycho_Brahe.

2. See Gen. 17:4–5.

3. See 2 Cor. 3:18 KJV.

4. See Gen. 31:19.

5. See John 15:18–25.

6. See John 8:56–59.

7. See John 1:1–3; Col. 1:15–17.

## Chapter 2 A Pilgrim—or a Drifter?

1. John Bunyan, *The Pilgrim's Progress: From This World to That Which Is to Come*, part one, sec. 216, Gutenberg Ebook, accessed March 17, 2019, https://www.gutenberg.org/files/131/131-h/131-h.htm.

2. Bunyan, *The Pilgrim's Progress*, sec. 221.

3. See esp. Heb. 11:8–13 KJV.

4. Tamara M. Green, *The City of the Moon God: Religious Traditions of Harran* (New York: Brill, 1992), 21.

5. Michael Catt, *The Power of Surrender: Breaking Through to Revival* (Nashville: B&H, 2010), 105.

6. Charles Simpson, *Walking in the Footsteps of David Wilkerson: The Journey and Reflections of a Spiritual Son* (Shippensburg, PA: Destiny Image, 2018), 175.

7. Watchmen on the Wall, "Prayer Targets: NDP; Military Sexual Assault, Low Morale, Women in Combat; SCOTUS, Israel; More," Family Research Council, May 6, 2015, https://www.frc.org/get.cfm?i=PW15E01.

8. Watchmen on the Wall, "Prayer Targets."

9. Watchmen on the Wall, "Prayer Targets."

## Chapter 3 A Failure of Faith

1. David Roper, "God Loves You," sermon delivered at Peninsula Bible Church, Palo Alto, California, November 2, 1975, LDolphin.org, September 7, 2000, http://ldolphin.org/roper/malachi/pdf/3445.pdf.

2. Mark Hopkins, "The Down-Grade Controversy," Christian History Institute, accessed March 17, 2019, https://christianhistoryinstitute.org/magazine/article/down-grade-controversy.

## Chapter 4 God's Promise Renewed

1. Associated Press, "The Recluse," *News-Press* (Ft. Myers, FL), January 9, 1978, 13.

2. See Matt. 26:17–29.

3. Ashton Applewhite, William R. Evans III, and Andrew Frothingham, *And I Quote: The Definitive Collection of Quotes, Sayings, and Jokes for the Contemporary Speech Maker* (New York: St. Martin's Press, 1992), 124.

## Chapter 5 The God Who Makes Covenants

1. Antonia Fraser, *Cromwell: The Lord Protector* (New York: Grove Press, 1973), 38.

2. William Fields, *The Scrap-Book: Consisting of Tales and Anecdotes, Biographical, Historical, Patriotic, Moral, Religious, and Sentimental Pieces in Prose and Poetry* (Philadelphia: Lippincott, 1857), 540.

3. Chantal Wright, *Literary Translation* (New York: Routledge, 2016), 30.

4. See Rom. 8:31–39.

## Chapter 6 The Chapter of Failure

1. James Barron, "Train Kills 9 Teen-Agers on L.I. as Van Goes Past Crossing Gate," *New York Times*, March 15, 1982, https://www.nytimes.com/1982/03/15/nyregion/train-kills-9-teen-agers-on-li-as-van-goes-past-crossing-gate.html.

## Chapter 7 The Silence of God

1. See Luke 18:1–8.

## Chapter 8 The Friend of God

1. See Gen. 5:24; Heb. 11:5.

2. Jeffrey S. Nevid and Spencer A. Rathus, *Psychology and the Challenges of Life, Binder Ready Version: Adjustment and Growth* (Hoboken, NJ: Wiley, 2016), 344.

3. See Matt. 5:13–16.

4. See Matt. 24, esp. v. 8.

## Chapter 9 The Birth of Laughter

1. Norman Cousins, *Head First: The Biology of Hope and the Healing Power of the Human Spirit* (New York: Penguin, 1989), 126.

2. Federation of American Societies for Experimental Biology, "Body's Response to Repetitive Laughter Is Similar to the Effect of Repetitive Exercise, Study Finds," ScienceDaily, April 26, 2010, https://www.sciencedaily.com/releases/2010/04/100426113058.htm.

3. Michal Kranz, "Polls Show That Republicans and Democrats Are More Divided Than Ever Before," Business Insider, October 6, 2017, https://www.businessinsider.com/pew-research-polls-democrats-republicans-divided-2017-10.

## Chapter 10 Abraham's Stars

1. Sam Harris, *Letter to a Christian Nation* (New York: Knopf, 2006), ix.

2. See Matt. 5:9, 43–45.

3. Qur'an 8:12, The Quranic Arabic Corpus, Shakir translation, accessed January 30, 2019, http://corpus.quran.com/translation.jsp?chapter=8&verse=12.

4. Qur'an 9:29, The Quranic Arabic Corpus, Shakir translation, accessed January 30, 2019, http://corpus.quran.com/translation.jsp?chapter=9&verse=29.

5. Richard Dawkins, *The God Delusion* (New York: Houghton Mifflin, 2008), chap. 9: "Childhood, Abuse and the Escape from Religion," especially his discussion of Nicholas Humphrey's 1997 Amnesty Lecture, pp. 366–79.

6. Christopher Hitchens, *god Is Not Great: How Religion Poisons Everything* (New York: Twelve/Hachette, 2007), 207.

7. Dawkins, *The God Delusion*, 274.

8. Dawkins, *The God Delusion*, 274–75.

**Michael Youssef** is the founder and president of Leading The Way with Dr. Michael Youssef (www.LTW.org), a worldwide ministry that leads the way for people living in spiritual darkness to discover the light of Christ through the creative use of media and on-the-ground ministry teams. His weekly television programs and daily radio programs are broadcast in twenty-five languages and seen worldwide, airing more than twelve thousand times per week. He is also the founding pastor of The Church of The Apostles in Atlanta, Georgia, with more than three thousand members. Youssef was born in Egypt and lived in Lebanon and Australia before coming to the United States. In 1984, he fulfilled a childhood dream of becoming an American citizen. He holds degrees from Moore College in Sydney, Australia, and Fuller Theological Seminary in California. In 1984, he earned a PhD in social anthropology from Emory University. He and his wife live in Atlanta and have four grown children and ten grandchildren.

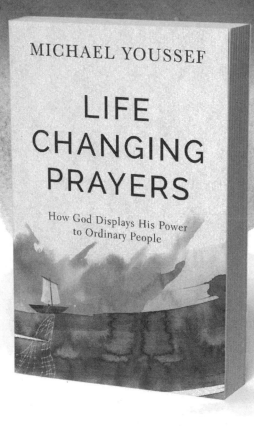

# Connect with
# Dr. Michael Youssef!

## MichaelYoussef.com

# Biblical Encouragement for You—Anytime, Anywhere

Leading The Way with Dr. Michael Youssef is passionately proclaiming uncompromising Truth through every major form of media, empowering you to know and follow Christ. There are many FREE ways you can connect with Dr. Youssef's teachings:

- Thousands of sermons and articles online
- TV and radio programs worldwide
- Apps for your phone or tablet
- A monthly magazine, and more!

# A movement is growing— and hundreds of thousands of souls are coming to faith in Jesus Christ.

**66** Thank you for sending a pastor my way. He counseled me after I was about to put an end to my life. <u>I accepted the Lord Jesus along with my brother</u>. . . . Now I know why I watched your broadcast at the right time. My life is for Jesus from now on. **99**

— SYRIA

From closed countries in the Middle East to right here in America, God is drawing souls to Christ through the ministry of Leading The Way with Dr. Michael Youssef.

You can join Leading The Way on the front lines of gospel ministry— producing biblical teaching programs in new languages, discipling former Muslims coming to faith in closed countries, and helping Christians impact their communities for Christ.

➡ **Learn more and partner with us today at LTW.org.**